D1552205

CLASSIC MODERN HOUSES IN EUROPE

CLASSIC MODERN HOUSES IN EUROPE

RICHARD EINZIG

NA
7325
.E369

The Architectural Press . London

ACKNOWLEDGEMENTS

INDIANA
PURDUE
LIBRARY
SEP 1 7 1982
FORT WAYNE

WITHDRAWN

I would like to thank the architects and designers whose works are shown in this collection for their help, and for their co-operation in making available drawings and information. (Even in some cases for their assistance in moving heavy photographic equipment from view to view!)

Grateful thanks also to the house owners and their families for allowing disruption of their lives during two or three days of camera activity, to the extent in three instances of re-furnishing major spaces in their houses; and for their great hospitality. To my dark-room and office staff and in particular to my wife, all thanks for their terrific back-up assistance over the years which it has taken to build up this collection of houses.

Lastly, I would like to express my grateful appreciation of my godmother, Wilma Hilary Jones. Without her encouragement, back in 1957, it is unlikely that any of the photographs in this book would have existed.

Title page illustration: Pavilion house and Japanese gardens at Shipton-under-Wychwood, Oxfordshire.
Architects: Stout and Litchfield
Pages 6/7: Farmer's solar-heated house at Fluy, Picardy.
Architects: Ian Ritchie and J. Van Den Bossche
Opposite: Barn-roof house near Barnstaple, Devonshire.
Architect: Peter Aldington

First published in 1981 by
The Architectural Press Ltd: London

© Renate Einzig 1981

ISBN 0 85139 479 5

All rights reserved. No part of this publication may be reproduced, stored in a retrieval system, or transmitted, in any form or by any means, electronic, mechanical, photocopying, recording or otherwise, without the prior permission, of the publishers. Such permission, if granted, is subject to a fee depending on the nature of the use

Set in 9 on 11pt Univers by Diemer & Reynolds Ltd, Bedford

Printed by Mackays of Chatham Ltd

CONTENTS

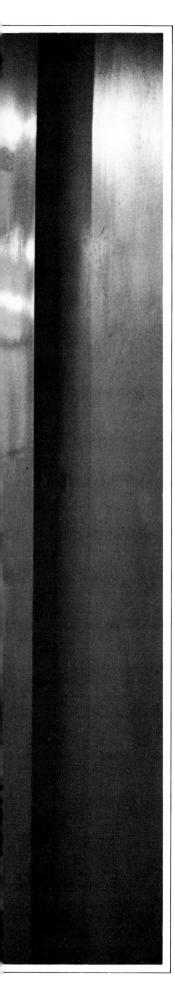

The history of modern architecture, its roots, diversity and contradictions can be traced through a study of its houses. Often a vehicle for exploring ideas in microcosm, the house is probably still the most exacting of design challenges.

It is interesting to contemplate the rich mixture of early seminal buildings, surprisingly diverse given so many common denominators. A range that encompasses the early courtyard house projects of Mies with their built reality in the Barcelona Pavilion, the organic forms of Frank Lloyd Wright's Falling Water, the stretched white skins and planes of Corbusier's Villa Stein at Garches, the hard-edged translucency of Chareau's Maison de Verre and the design science visions of Buckminster Fuller's Dymaxion House — all within the same few years' time span. Likewise, nearly two decades later, Philip Johnson's glass pavilion in New Canaan is contemporary with the rough hewn arched fortress of Maison Jaoul and the toyland ad hocery of the Eames House. These intrinsic differences transcend national and regional boundaries, tempting though it is to explain such diversity by West Coast/East Coast or American/European polarities.

Moving on into the sixties and the seventies, the European emphasis of this book is appropriately visual and the images tell the story of diverse trends better than any written treatise on the subject. The variations on the theme of the house are wide ranging and seem more philosophical than geographical in their origins. A number of familiar mainstreams are evident, some rooted in a nostalgic view of the traditional past, others in an optimistic view of a more technological future. It is interesting to contemplate what future volumes of such a book might show. The possibilities of a true vernacular might emerge from the challenge of having to take a more global view of energy, perhaps in the direction of Buckminster Fuller's optimistic and egalitarian vision of the 'air deliverable, sewer-and-water-mains-emancipated, energy-harvesting and dwelling machine' achieved by 'the highest aeronautical and engineering facilities of the world redirected from weaponry to "livingry" production' with its implications of 'an unprecedentedly higher standard of living for all than has ever been experienced by any, able to live entirely on its sun-energy-derived income'. Or will such future volumes reveal more élitist retreats into historical, so-called vernacular styling as a kind of Luddite reaction in the face of the apparent threat of rapid change? Either way, it seems very likely on past precedent that any new directions or shifts of emphasis, whether technological or philosophical are most likely to be pioneered initially on the smaller-scale opportunities presented by the dwelling.

For many of us current insights and historical hindsights rely on communication through the medium of photography. The acceptance and eventual dependence on the camera since the nineteenth century is now almost taken for granted. Even so, it is worth reminding ourselves of the camera's power to recall by comparing Delamotte's photographs of the Crystal Palace in the 1850s with contemporary engravings of the period.

If photography is now accepted as a vehicle to chart visually the dry objective bones of historical evolution, then further questions are inevitably raised about the camera's ability to communicate the spirit of buildings — notwithstanding the uniqueness of architecture as a total three-dimensional art. If a house tells us about the owners and their architects, then in a similar manner the photograph tells us more than we probably care to admit about the individual behind the camera.

During the period in which the book was prepared, Richard Einzig fell the victim of an illness from which he subsequently died in July 1980 — a tragic and irreplaceable loss. He was a perfectionist and craftsman who, with his wife Renate, insisted on personal control over the total process from visiting the building to the production of final photographic prints. His sensitivity to the spirit of a building and its site context was matched by a highly selective eye and a mastery of the technical means. The pursuit of perfection and a refusal to compromise are rare qualities indeed, especially when combined with the kind of quiet and unassuming air which was special to Richard. This book was intended to be the first in a series — sadly it is now an end in itself, for how many are there left who can so faithfully capture the true spirit of architecture and reproduce it with such loving technical care? Richard Einzig's photographs are an inspiration to photographers and architects alike.

SHINGLE-CLAD HOUSE

LAKE COMO

ARCHITECT
Marco Zanuso

STRUCTURAL ENGINEER
Norbert Wackernell

'A site in a million' is what most town house owners would consider this situation—probably most country house owners, too. It is set back 30 yards or so from the edge of Lake Como, with only a grassy meadow and a row of small trees between it and the shore, with the slopes of a range of lower Alps rising immediately behind the site and views across the lake to the high Alps.

The owner of the site, an industrial designer, and his family, had any number of reasons for wishing to build and live here for as much of the year as city schooling and intercontinental business travel would allow. Possibilities for walking, climbing, swimming (Lake Como here is clear and clean again), skiing locally or at St Moritz, only a two-hour drive distant: all these were factors. But the major consideration was the winds. Lake Como is situated in such a geographical position that, virtually at any time of any day, the particular wind of one's choice may be found somewhere on it: predictably. For this keen sailing family, it had to be a Lake Como site for their house.

As architect, a friend was chosen, Professor Marco Zanuso, also deeply involved in industrial design, and with a very active and well-known practice in Milan. Being in the design field, the architect's client and his wife both had strong views on their proposed house. The instructions received by Zanuso, who also knows the Lake Como environment extremely well, were therefore comprehensive.

A house was to be created allowing views to the north and south ends of the lake from within the house, as well as of the upper parts of the mountains behind it, but at the same time shielding the interior as completely as possible from the noise of motor traffic on the nearby road, and also from views of other detached buildings both on the slopes behind the site and some 30 yards away to either side.

The interior accommodation was to include one parents' bedroom, well separated visually and acoustically from a children's area containing three study-bedrooms; parent and child areas were each to have their own bathroom; and there was to be a guest bedroom with space for adding a bathroom en-suite with it at a later date. The main living, dining and kitchen spaces were to be in a large and open-plan area, and this part of the interior was to be capable of being opened up easily to the garden and fresh air of the scenic spaces beyond.

A really snug 'bad weather living-room' with an open fireplace (to supplement overall oil-fired central hot water radiator heating) was also required, as well as a study for the client, and a full plan basement for boat maintenance and general storage and a children's hobby workshop. The structure of the house was to be wood, and it was to have exterior and interior finishes in wood.

The plan chosen, an angled L, with its inner walls glazed (armour plate glass for security) has covered, except in two aspects, all the requirements of the client as originally conceived: views to the mountains behind the house have been kept to a minimum in the interests of sound insulation; the material of the main structure was reconsidered, because, for the high, wide-span open roof and unimpeded floor spaces visualised, together with 'hung' gallery accommodation, a solely wooden structure would have needed substantial and deep sectioned beams with stabilising cross members. The client decided against such a complex and massive visual effect. Accordingly, structural engineer Dr Norbert Wackernell was consulted and asked to provide a slimmed down structural design. Such a result he achieved very successfully by means of an unobtrusive steel frame structure.

The client had also expressed a wish for the material of the external walls to be identical to that of the roof. Cedar shingles were the chosen answer; as is usual, these have been allowed to weather untreated, and after only two years the house already appears to be merging into the landscape.

From the road entrance only the top parts of the shingle walls are visible (the downward slope of the roof towards the lake following the ground slope hides it completely from this direction) and the house can easily be mistaken for a two-dimensional high fence. As one approaches down the slope, the first surprise comes in the realisation that here is a three-dimensional enclosure. The second surprise comes as one moves into this enclosure through a modest front door in the 'fence'; the feeling that the volume of the main interior space is far greater than one would imagine from looking at the outside. From this one can appreciate the enigmatic relationship between the interior scale of this house, relative to the human beings in it, and the exterior scale relative to the high mountain and wide lake environment in which this house is set.

A house with a quietly unobtrusive exterior in which the scale, space and uplift of its environment are mirrored in the interior.

1 View from the south-east with the house set on the slopes of a lower Alpine meadow

2 Looking out from the living space to the panoramic view across and along Lake Como to the high mountains beyond

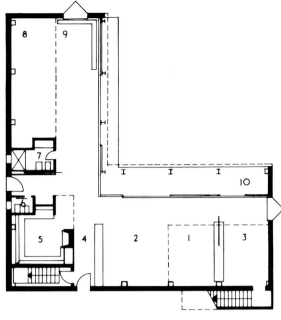

SHINGLE-CLAD
HOUSE,
LAKE COMO:
Ground floor
1 living room
2 dining area
3 study
4 kitchen
5 snuggery
6 wc
7 shower
8 children's bedrooms
9 play area
10 terrace

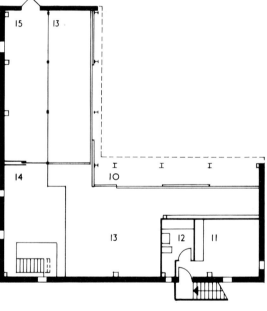

First floor
11 master bedroom
12 bathroom
13 void
14 gallery
15 guest rooms

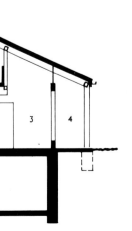

Section
1 master bedroom
2 study
3 living room
4 terrace
5 cellar
6 stairs to bedroom

3 *The main living/dining/kitchen space. The large volume of this space, as approached here from the entrance hall, produces a sense of surprise after the apparently smaller scale of the exterior*

4 *A detail of the east corner, also showing two of the bay windows which are fully glazed for maximum views to the mountains*
5 *The south corner of the house, with magnificent views across Lake Como towards the higher Alps*

6

7

6 The main living space at night. The steel-frame structure has allowed this roof volume to be free of cross beams and ties

7 The free-standing kitchen storage and work counter; behind this, the sink unit recess with full-height sliding door for immediate hiding of clutter

8 The approach from the west showing the interesting two-dimensional illusion which the house presents from this aspect. The necessary wide-angle view, though still impressive, minimises the real height of the mountains and the scale of this environment

8

HILL RESIDENCE

NEAR REUTLINGEN, BADEN-WÜRTTEMBERG

ARCHITECT
Wilfried Beck-Erlang

SITE ARCHITECT
W. Pfeiffer

STRUCTURAL ENGINEER
Ing. Büro Bauer

1 *The tough-looking south-west elevation, to the road. Note the carefully landscaped flight of steps to the main entrance and the three-car garage door*

Reutlingen is a south German town near Stuttgart. It has a thriving textile industry and lies at the edge of the range of high hills (up to 3000 ft/1000 m) known as the Schwäbische Alb. On one of these foothills, about 3 miles/5 km from the centre of Reutlingen, a local industrialist acquired a very fine west-facing site with views across the River Neckar valley. The land was scheduled for low density residential development. The owner took the unusual step, with a private house project, of holding a limited competition. Five architects were invited to prepare schemes and Wilfried Beck-Erlang's was chosen to be built.

The requirements of the client were, basically, for a house providing the necessary accommodation for his family with three children, incorporating a swimming pool, a housekeeper flat and a three-car

garage.

The architect's very interesting and complex plan evolved around the second-level living areas. At this level a large open paved terrace was created. It was oriented to catch the sun and had built-in seating plus barbecue, hollowed cave-like from the hill. Facing south onto this terrace was the swimming pool with changing accommodation, sauna, and a separate après sauna court sunk into the hillside. To the left of the swimming pool is the south-east facing fully glazed entrance wall of the casual-living space, off which, through a sliding wall, is the dining-room with kitchen beyond.

A half-level down, and open above the balcony wall to the upper living space, is a more formal and impressive double-height sitting area. Both from this space and from a small terrace which leads off it, the

wide views and sunsets can be enjoyed throughout the year. A half-level up from the second level is a mezzanine gallery library projecting into the lower sitting space and with views down into it and the casual-living space.

The bedroom zone is on the third level under the roof. This sculptural slate roof is a major feature of the building. With its vertical fascias of the same material it seems to flow gracefully into the transition from roof to boarded concrete or glass wall; from certain aspects a most dramatic 'hooded' appearance has been achieved; mainly boarded on the underside, it 'floats' over the glazing in the formal sitting space, the main staircase and other areas; projecting beyond the walls for some feet, it gives weather protection to many parts of the balconies and terraces. Its use of black slate has been echoed

in the slate floor slabs of the living areas and staircase.

A further very carefully conceived aspect of the planning was the possibility for inside/outside living and circulation. The roof of the swimming pool forms a terrace with access from the bedrooms, and a staircase link down to the main second-level terrace; this in turn is linked by a staircase to a lower terrace with access to the lower living spaces.

Looking down at the house from higher up the slope and particularly from the south, the impression with eyes half closed is of a smoothly surfacing science fiction object. With eyes open one sees a tough yet elegant example of modern country house architecture, beautifully detailed and built, which functions well and which has fully justified the owner's decision to hold a competition.

2 Dusk view of the main staircase elevation from an upper ground-floor balcony, providing an interesting contrast of solid and transparency

3 (overleaf) View of the upper part of the house with its dramatic and sculptural slate roof from the steeply sloping lawns to the south. At camera level are the glazed wall to the swimming pool and the main terrace. There is a glimpse of the view out across the River Neckar valley

2

3

HILL RESIDENCE NEAR REUTLINGEN:
Section

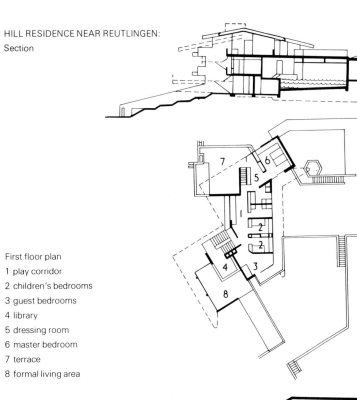

First floor plan
1 play corridor
2 children's bedrooms
3 guest bedrooms
4 library
5 dressing room
6 master bedroom
7 terrace
8 formal living area

Ground floor plan
1 informal sitting room
1A formal living area
2 dining room
3 swimming pool
4 sauna
5 sauna terrace
6 store
7 main terrace

Lower ground floor
1 entrance hall
2 caretaker
3 wine cellar
4 hobby room
5 storage
6 bar
7 boiler room
8 oil store

4 *The air-conditioned swimming pool seen from the main terrace, with the ceiling and walls of sealed pine boarding. The roof of this forms one of the linked terraces*

5 *Looking towards the north-west corner, the building takes an imposingly craggy form and* silhouette. *Note the rainwater drainage spouts which project well to avoid splashes on the building*

6 *An interesting comparison with the dusk shot 2, with the reversal of the dark and light toned areas. The large scale of this building is indicated by the figure at ground level. The view is from the master bedroom terrace*

7

8

7 Detail of a drainage spout and hand-
forged chain from the main roof.
These projections help to give the roof
its rather menacing hooded
appearance. At camera level, the
glazing at the left is to the casual living
area; ahead, to the swimming pool

8 Detail on the library/staircase
landing, with the bookshelf ends fixed
into the concrete

9 A view into the double-height formal
sitting area from the balcony of the
main living space. The gallery at the
top right is the library. Splendid view
out to the west from this room, its
balcony and terrace. The roof
'floating' out over the glazing has a
glued laminated timber beam
structure

10 The master bedroom with the door
open to the upper terrace serving all
four bedrooms on this level. An
external staircase leads to the lower
main terrace and swimming pool

11 The dining room, open in this view
to the main staircase and informal
living space, can be closed off by the
sliding wall, seen to the left. To the
right of the curtain in the background
is the balcony to the lower living space

9

MULTI-PAVILION COURTYARD HOUSE
IN THE SOMERSET HILLS

ARCHITECT
Stout & Litchfield

The estate of Somerton Erleigh has been owned by the family of Mr A. R. E. Pretor-Pinney since about 1795; its name can, in fact, be traced back at least to 1186, probably to AD894. In 1962 the main house on the estate was sold, being too large and inconvenient for domestic use today, but the Pretor-Pinneys retained the name 'Somerton Erleigh', to be used for a new house in due course. In this apparently unusual step they were really following earlier precedent, since the location of the manor house of the estate has been changed twice before in its history.

The site for the new Somerton Erleigh was chosen for its commanding position on a wooded ridge overlooking a foreground of 18th-century landscape, with views to the lovely, rolling Somerset hills beyond.

Mr Pretor-Pinney's aim and the instructions given to architects Stout and Litchfield were that the new house should provide a focus and act as a repository for the historical name, while being a convenient and modern family house. A grand house was not required, but rather a complex of buildings of moderate size, quite spread out but nevertheless forming a very decided whole. The look of the outside, including a visually satisfying pattern of roofs was important. A successor in miniature to a Roman Villa, mediaeval manor and Georgian country house was suggested.

The earlier houses by the same architects at Shipton-under-Wychwood, Oxfordshire (illustrated on pages 140-3) and Bishopswood Road, Highgate, had explored the ideas of linked groups of pitched roofed pavilions and two-way lighting roof-windows, and in both instances the informal effect of a sloping ridge resulting from the introduction of a non-right angle in the plan forms. These ideas were expanded at Somerton Erleigh.

Bearing in mind the Roman villa suggestion in the brief, the architects started out with the atrium, or courtyard, as the centre of the house, providing a sheltered, roofless living-room. The four main covered elements of the house, the living-room, the dining-room/kitchen, the playroom and children's bedrooms and principal bedrooms were each to occupy one side of the courtyard and visually open to it in varying degrees according to the privacy required. A flat-roofed, glazed 'cloister' would immediately enclose the courtyard and extend into circulation and subsidiary spaces between the main pavilions, culminating at the main entrance lobby.

As built, the pavilions take different but similar forms according to their use and position. For example, the living-room is a room with double aspect, to the east the view and to the west the sun

and the courtyard. It therefore has a double-pitch roof with east and west-facing clerestory and main windows, while the study/estate office, which required seclusion from the family part of the house, only faces outwards towards the view and only has a one-way pitch to the roof.

1 *The central courtyard seen from the dining-room. View across to the roofs of the guest and master bedrooms*

The rooms in each pavilion are so placed on the cloister circulation as to provide close associations: living to dining/kitchen, to playroom/children's bedrooms, to parents' bedroom, to guest room, to living-room. Within each pavilion associated functions are grouped: dining-room and kitchen and

playroom and children's bedrooms. Conversely non-related functions are as far removed from each other as possible, with the playroom far from the formal living-room.

The study/estate office and the garage extend the composition beyond the mere formality of the courtyard group.

On the constructional side, the walls of the house are of cavity construction with the outer skin of second-hand blue lias stone largely obtained from a nearby ruined walled garden. The inner skin is of insulating concrete block, plastered and white painted.

The pitched roofs are timber substructure with natural Welsh slates and finished internally with varnished Columbian Pine boarding. There is a 3 in glass wool insulation and vapour barrier above the boarding. The ceilings slope with the roof pitch. The flat roofs are weatherproofed with asphalt.

The floor is a concrete substructure with an insulated and heated screed with a heather brown quarry tile finish. All windows are double glazed and large windows open by sliding horizontally. The furniture is Form International — Charles Eames inside, Verner Panton plastic chairs outside.

Central heating is provided by underfloor circulation of hot water through copper pipes. Heating and domestic hot water are from an oil-fired boiler.

The approach to the house is romantic: along a lane, then up a rising, curving drive as the house slowly appears above the brow of the hill. At first, apparently a random collection of irregularly shaped roofs and stone walls, suggestive even at a distance of some kind of very well-built farm complex; then the awareness that there is much more to it than meets the eye at first sight. The randomness becomes less so, as one approaches. The consistent use of materials and the precise way in which they have been fitted together to form this multi-pavilion house becomes more apparent, but the complexity is still there, even when one has penetrated the entrance hall and reached the elegant interior with its Charles Eames furniture. Only a study of the plan reveals the formal logic of the design. The visitor can but be dazzled and excited by the angles, the bright airy atmosphere, the sparkle at night, the vistas from pavilion through court to pavilion and out to the hills and the cows.

A Roman villa? It could be, with its courtyard. A mediaeval manor? Certainly robust enough. A Georgian country house? Great for parties. But this boisterous house, this architecture, is better than all these: it has the rare attribute of being *fun* to be in.

2

3

4

2 In the centre of the picture, the 'cloister' circulation around the courtyard, here forming part of the living-room. Daylight coming into this space from four different directions produces an ever-changing bright and airy feeling

3 Skyline composition from the south-west. The roofs appear more random than from many directions, but whatever the view, the roof composition is tremendous visual fun. The idea of the linked group of pitched-roof but sloping ridge

pavilions has apparently been taken as far as it can go. Unless the architects know better

4 Dusk — and sparkling illumination of the courtyard. Looking here from the playroom across to the living-room and out to the distant trees and hills

5 A night view of the dining-room from the south-west 'cloister'. The storage screen to the kitchen is at the left. The table and chairs were designed by Charles Eames

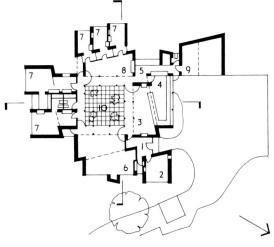

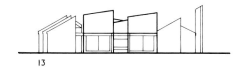

13

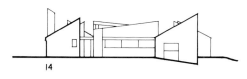

14

11

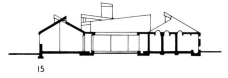

15

12

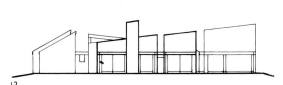

16

COURTYARD HOUSE IN SOMERSET

1 entrance hall
2 administration office
3 dining room
4 kitchen
5 utility
6 living room
7 bedrooms
8 playroom
9 garage
10 courtyard
11 South-west elevation
12 North-east elevation
13 South-east elevation
14 North-west elevation
15 section A-A
16 section B-B

6

7

6 *Not a view normally seen, but well worth capturing to show the careful way in which the striking but complex arrangement of sloping and flat (circulation) roofs with clerestory glazing has been designed. Looking north-east*

7 *The long master bedroom viewed through its south-east facing window wall, with the courtyard in the background. High ceilings with angled boarding and sloping ridges and one wall on a splay make this room a fascinating microcosm of the whole house*

8 *Looking up the meadow to the house on the ridge. With apparently random, farm-like roofs, it sits superbly in its pastoral landscape and commands splendid views out from that exposed position*

8

BARN-ROOF HOUSE
NEAR BARNSTAPLE, DEVONSHIRE

ARCHITECT
Peter Aldington of Aldington,
Craig & Collinge

Goodleigh, a small village in Devonshire some four miles from the town of Barnstaple on the River Taw estuary, was chosen by a local professional man and his wife for the site of their new house. Having known architect Peter Aldington for many years, and thinking most highly of his work, they decided that, regardless of the travel costs of site supervision involved in each of his 350 mile round journeys from Buckinghamshire, he must be the right architect for them.

As always, very keen to maintain full control of the building work, but with too many commitments for a small-scale job requiring distant site visits, the architect hit on the idea of *a* having the entire timber part of the structure locally made in Oxford, where frequent supervisory visits would be possible, and *b* making use of a simple hip roof structure supported by posts and twin beams, which could be set up and tiled—to form a 'barn'—before the rest of the wooden structure and joinery was transported from Oxford. Once the posts were accurately positioned, all the setting out and building from then on could be simply related to them by the local building contractor with a minimum of architect's supervision and all under cover. An ideal, logical, professional solution, satisfying both client and architect.

The site for the house was on the edge of the hilly village, adjoining farm land, secluded and with splendid views over the valley and rolling hillsides. The brief for the architect was that full advantage was to be taken of the views; that the living, dining, kitchen and entrance areas could all be open plan but with some kind of division to reduce any effect of barrenness, and the dining area should be small and cosy. The three-bedroom accommodation was to be private and insulated acoustically. The house was to be easy to run and clean. Finally—and a touch of magic was clearly required to satisfy this part of the brief—a study area was requested which was not to be, as is usual, cut off from all the active part of the house, but which would be a sort of open alcove in the middle of the living area; however, the inevitable clutter of papers and books was not to be generally visible to people outside the study.

Aldington and Craig have a rare ability and wish to design their buildings to harmonise with the local environment. This one was to be no exception and a study of Devon farm buildings showed that many of them had slated roofs and were set low into the landscape or hugged closely to the sides of the hills.

A similar treatment was applied here, the house being dug well in; and from the road entrance the long roof ridge, although over 17 ft high from livingroom floor level, is still well below the horizon line. Grey concrete tiles were used rather than

extremely expensive slate. The tiles also allow a lower pitch roof.

As in the other pitched-roof houses by the same architect, designed over the last 17 years, much of the roof space has been left open. In this case the volumes flow from space to space with greater smoothness than before, perhaps because the structure in the roof has been hidden with a cladding of Douglas Fir ply, and the whole roof on its deep edge beams has been allowed to 'float' over a narrow ribbon of clerestory glazing, which continues into glazed gable ends. The words of the architect describe his planning conception further:

The posts and beams establish a grid completely covered by the roof. The accommodation is defined below by free-form rectilinear or circular areas of block or glass which pierce or run with the grid. Wherever they do pierce the grid, however, internally or externally, they have a form of sub-roof which returns, glazed or decked, to a clerestory glazed 7 ft 3 in datum line rigidly controlled by the grid. This condition is adhered to in all but one important exception—in the centre of the house—and produces a peculiarly pleasant inside/outside confusion, which increases the involvement with the landscape.

The exception is the lower level blockwork forming the study-booth/poop/control centre/watch tower which is set centrally among the open-plan spaces as required in the brief. In its position raised well above the sitting space floor and with views out through the fully-glazed south-west end of the house, it can feel like any of these four, depending on the mood of the occupier. This space has not only solved the requirements of the brief but has, it seems, provided bonus benefits.

The living space with its Form International furniture, has been sunk down about 2 ft below the rest of the house, to follow the levels of the site down the slope and provide, physically with the glazed doors open, and the Wheatley Golden Brown quarry tile floor continuing onto the terrace, and visually through the fixed glazing, the pleasant—very pleasant indeed—inside/outside confusion referred to in the architect's statement.

This large open-plan volume, in particular, and the house as a whole are a fascinatingly successful and three dimensionally imaginative combination of the materials concrete block, glass and wood.

The clients are more than pleased that they took the risk of those long supervision journeys and say that they have been given what they now realise they wanted all along; a comprehensive brief from them helped. But so did that touch of magic.

1 The main entrance porch at night, showing the translucent fibre glass glazed sub-roof and panels to either side of the diagonal boarded, pivoted front door. Note the excellent detail of the sunken door mat, something rarely seen

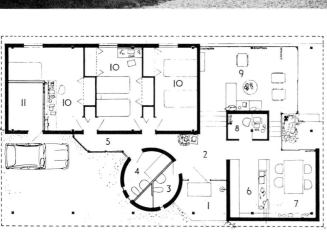

HOUSE, GOODLEIGH, BARNSTAPLE:

ground floor plan	6 kitchen
1 porch	7 dining room
2 hall	8 office
3 cloakroom	9 living room
4 bathroom	10 bedrooms
5 bedroom lobby	11 store-room

2 *The house tucked into its Devonshire hill as seen from the site entrance, looking south-west over the stunning views commanded by the site. It is astonishing how much more spacious the interior is than seems possible from its exterior*

3 *The thoughtfully lit bathroom in its semi-circular tower. The loft above contains the cold water cistern. At the right is one of the translucent glazed fibre glass panels which fronts onto the car port*

4 *Looking into the living space from the terrace entrance, at night. In the centre left is the study, set centrally in the living activity zone, as required in the brief. The steps at the right are to the entrance hall; those at the left, to the dining space. The chairs are by Charles Eames*

5 *A night view of the elegant living space at the end of the south elevation. The moulded plastic chairs outside are by Verner Panton*

6 *The end of the open kitchen seen from the dining area with its low ceiling. A marvellous sense of airy flowing space in this view right along the length of the house. The study, 'in the middle of it all', with its door slightly open, is to the right of the picture; doors off to the bedrooms in the centre*

4

6

7 *West elevation seen from the terrace with the projecting end of the inside/outside living area ahead; glazed door to dining area at the left*

8 *Looking from the study/booth to the excellently detailed kitchen and the dining area. Note the disciplined continuation of horizontals in different planes and the glazed gable end, which allows the required low sub-roof to the dining area*

9 *The view over the rock-pool at night really shows the transparency and sparkle of the west end of the house*

10 *View over the dining table to the terrace at the right; living space, centre; enclosed yet open study, and kitchen work unit to the left. The low ceiling to the dining space was specifically required by the brief. This end of the house has a splendid view out to the hills. The simply expressed timber structure and the floating effect of the main roof over the clerestory glazing are well shown*

9

7

8

10

VERNACULAR COASTAL HOUSING

LES MARINES DE COGOLIN, NEAR ST TROPEZ

ARCHITECT
ATEAO, Project directed by
Jean Dimitrijevic
SOFIREV

Set on the Golfe de St Tropez between the lively and popular neo-Venetian 'lagoon town' of Port Grimaud and St Tropez itself, two miles' distant, Les Marines de Cogolin was built as a speculative development. A building company SOFIREV was formed on the initiative of the Banque Rothschild and the Compagnie Financière de Suez, in co-operation with Crédit Lyonnais, the Compagnie Générale Trans-atlantique and the Chargeurs Réunis. With such a collection of financial bodies to keep happy, all credit to the architects, who have planned and executed an imaginative village complex, in style falling, one might say, half way between Port Grimaud and 'holiday coast international'. In other words, they have produced a completely modern coastal housing and marina environment which is really integrated into its Var setting close to such compact old hill-top towns as Gassin and Ramatuelle.

The basic requirement was for some 600 dwellings of different sizes, with accompanying shops, restaurants and a swimming pool. In the 76 acres of enclosed water, moorings were required for 1500 boats of from 8 to 35 m or larger. This density is, it is claimed, the lowest for any of the Côte d'Azur yachting ports. A centrally positioned Harbour Master's Office with all yachting administration services and a repair shipyard were also to be incorporated.

The solution which the architects chose was to divide the harbour into three basins, rather in the manner of the traditional Mediterranean fishing port, each with its own curving terraces of flats, maisonettes and houses set immediately behind the broad quays. This meant that the scale of each of the sub-villages, La Brigantine, La Galiote and La Cascadelle, could be kept compact, and walking distances from dwellings to boat berths held to a minimum. The exterior walls of the buildings have been treated in the local Provencal/Var manner, with rough rendering overall, including the splendid flat-top splayed chimney stacks/ventilation outlets, coloured light, ocre or pale pink. With the well-maintained surrounding low-spread planting plus bush and flower beds, set against the Mediterranean and its blue sky, these colours look absolutely right together with the roofs which are all covered with half-round 'Roman' tiles, in all shades of red-brown, mixed randomly. The exterior woodwork is in hardwood impregnated to withstand maritime atmospheric conditions, as are the draught-proofing and closing systems. The roughcast vernacular exteriors do tend to conceal the extremely high standard to which these buildings have been detailed and finished, a standard kept up in the berth facilities which include self-illuminated supply points for water, power and telephone.

It is a standard which is expected by the top executive or industrialist on the look-out for a permanent holiday home or somewhere to retire. With views along the coast to St Maxime and St Tropez and inland to the Maures hills and possibilities for sailing, power boating, water skiing, fishing, diving or walking in the hills, situated only 58 miles from the thrills of Monaco, what more could be desired? Right here they have created the ultimate environmental pleasure: dancing in the Galiote night club, barefoot, in three inches of glorious, warm Mediterranean sea water.

1 *View from an upper walkway in La Galiote across the yacht basin to the eastern end of the same complex*

2 *Looking along a first-floor approach 'street' to the flats and houses of La Galiote. These routes have continuously changing vistas, and glimpses of the red/brown roofs with the blue water beyond. The vernacular flat-top splayed chimney stacks are also ventilation outlets*

1

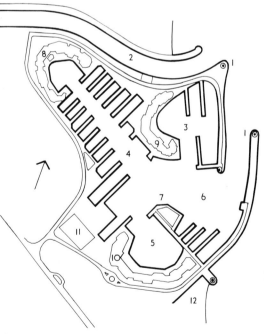

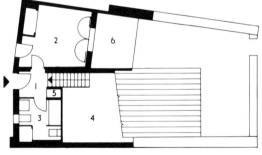

First floor plan

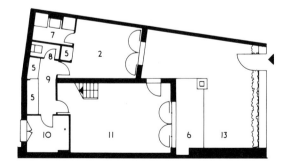

Ground floor plan

VERNACULAR COASTAL HOUSING	6 open harbour for short stay boats
ST TROPEZ: site plan	7 reception, the Harbour Master's office
1 lighthouse	8 La Cascadelle
2 La Giscle	9 La Brigantine
3 Bassin de la Brigantine	10 La Galiote
4 Bassin de la Cascadelle	11 yard
5 Bassin de la Galiote	12 beach

Ground floor plan	7 bathroom
1 entrance	8 wc
2 bedroom	9 landing
3 bathroom	10 kitchen
4 void over living room	11 living room
5 cupboards	12 terrace
6 terrace	13 garden

3 *Evening sun on the north-west face of La Brigantine, seen from its rival harbour, Port Grimaud, across the River Giscle*

4 *The quay side to the basin of La Brigantine, looking southwards. The extremely high standard to which these buildings have been detailed and finished is, probably deliberately, lost in the roughcast and excitingly modern yet Mediterranean idiom in which they have been massed*

5 *On the right of the picture, the western flank of La Galiote with its well-planted landscaping. Ahead to the north, over the open harbour waters, the curving terraced dwellings of La Brigantine; behind them, the Maures Hills. Note the exposed aggregate 'seats' at the edge of the broad quay: these are, in fact, well-disguised yacht supply points for water, power and telephone. They are even self-illuminated which indicates the standard to which this complex has been designed*

6 *A detail view of La Brigantine from its basin quayside. The irregular building groupings and staircases give continuous pleasure to the eye*

7 *View from the garden of a Type A ground-floor flat in La Cascadelle*

6

7

8 *The living-room of a sixth-floor penthouse maisonette in La Cascadelle, occupied by the family of a Swiss industrialist. The view is to the east, over the Cascadelle yacht basin to La Brigantine*

9 *Sliding window walls at either end allow excellent air circulation in this living-room of a flat in La Galiote. This view, from the terrace which faces the basin, indicates the standard of joinery and fittings. In the background is the private staircase down from the entrance gate to the secluded courtyard. On the right is the open-hearth fireplace for wood burning* 9

HOUSE WITH ART GALLERY

AT PILL CREEK, CORNWALL

ARCHITECTS
Richard Rogers & Partners
Foster Associates

LANDSCAPE ARCHITECTS
Southard and Branch

A dramatically steep tree-clad Cornish creek-side formed part of the site on which the architects for Marcus and Rene Brumwell were asked to design the house in this study. The accommodation was to include an open-plan living/dining/kitchen; a study, main bedroom, workshop and a fully self-contained guest suite. Full advantage was to be taken of the views and the house must, eventually if not immediately, integrate into its site to a high degree. Further requirements were that it should be easily extendable and that the maintenance requirement should be kept to the minimum. Finally, but by no means least important, the house was to have a scale appropriate to the display of the Brumwells' exceptional collection of modern paintings and sculpture, and their library of books.

To take advantage of the views over the trees, the architects positioned the house at the highest and flattest part of the site, just below the very minor coastal road. Noise from this would in any case be no problem as the intention was to have completely windowless walls facing in that direction. The most striking views towards the mouth of the creek and the sea were only visible from some 13 ft above ground level. It was therefore decided to position the living space at first-floor level and satisfy the brief for open-plan combination of this with the dining/library/kitchen in a vertical dimension instead of the usual horizontal. However, 'integration with the site' implied a long low building. The dilemma was solved by dividing the house into two visually separated wings, one with the accommodation just described, facing south, plus a roof top viewing deck, the other, for the remainder of the accommodation, single storey, facing west, plus a lower level boiler room built into the hillside. The wings follow the natural contours of the hill on two axes. Of these, one, external, runs east-west and leads from the off-road parking bay across a thin slab reinforced concrete bridge where the first of the many vistas starts; to the front door deck carefully placed in the 'neck' of the funnel-plan, shaped space between the wings; then down a grassed-tread concrete riser staircase with vistas forward and backwards (a delightful feel of Alvar Aalto's Saynätsalo about this) to the lawn and down ever steeper steps to the boathouse and creek.

The other axis, internal, runs south-north. It links all the rooms in the house, starting with the top roof deck, passing the living space which itself forms a deck open at front and back over the kitchen. It continues past the entrance hall, kinking down by the kitchen, tunnelling under the front door deck, turning again, into a long, light picture gallery with fully glazed roof through which external flood-lights stunningly illuminate this space at night. Off this gallery are the study, main bedroom and self-contained flat. All these have fully opening sliding walls facing onto the gallery, giving, as one moves through the space, a whole series of additional eye catching vistas into the different spaces, and beyond to views over and up the creek, through floor-to-ceiling glazing. The axis continues to the Hepworth sculpture at the far end of the gallery and as a footpath, through the garden to the underground garage at the north edge of the site. If necessary, an extension to the house could be made on to this end without problem.

Bearing in mind the 'minimum maintenance' requirements in the brief, the architects chose the following materials: for the walls inside and out, exposed honey-coloured Forticrete concrete blocks with matching mortar; for floors, Dorothea blue Welsh slate slabs with green and pink veins; for the exposed floor/roof slab soffits, honey-coloured ply shuttered poured concrete. Windows are frameless sliding, or with the fittings overall, anodised aluminium or stainless steel; the joinery is finished with a white plastic laminate or mirror glass; heating is from an oil-fired boiler producing hot air through structural ceiling ducts.

Integration into the local landscape is well advanced: creepers on the roofs are overgrowing the faces of the building, other plants are climbing up from the ground. Within a few years this house will, like a chameleon, have all but taken on the colouring and texture of its intentionally wild garden. This is what the Brumwells, long connected with Cornwall and its strong art life, wish to happen. But the internal and external vistas will remain to remind one that the architects have here resolved the planning and design requirements in a highly original and yet tremendously livable way.

1 *View from the first-floor front entrance, over the wall to the kitchen space and up the steps and round to the living space on the right*

2

2 *The steps seen in 1 with, beyond, a very steep staircase to the roof-top viewing deck, the south end of the north-south axis. To the right, the living-room*

3 *Looking back to the entrance hall from the steps to the living-room; below, the dining/kitchen space*

4 *The staircase from the ground floor to the first-floor entrance hall. At the right is the dining/kitchen space. The camera here is positioned under the deck outside the front door*

4

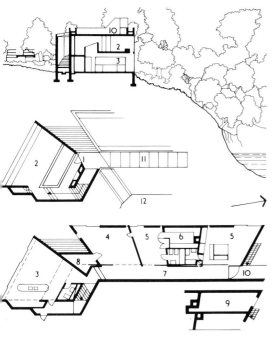

HOUSE WITH ART GALLERY,
CORNWALL: section
Second floor plan
First floor plan
1 entrance
2 living room
3 dining area/kitchen
4 study

5 bedroom
6 dressing room
7 gallery
8 store for paintings
9 boilers
10 terrace
11 skylights
12 parking

5 *The gallery living-room with a
glimpse of the view this room enjoys
through the window wall. Note the
thin mullions and framing*

6 *Looking from the master bedroom
to the picture gallery, at night. A fine
contrast and balance between rough,
smooth and soft materials*

7 *Night view looking into the
kitchen/dining space from its terrace.
Dramatic lighting and the confidently
curving stainless steel island unit, with
double height voids to either side, help
to make this space a memorable one
among modern house interiors*

8

9

10

11

8 *The beautifully lit picture gallery, at dusk. Off to the left, with their sliding partition walls open, are the study, master bedroom and the guest suite*

9 *Merging into its garden background, the planted roof of the bedroom wing as seen from the roof-top viewing deck. Note the visual simplicity of the detailing in contrast to the complex angles of the plan*

10 *The magnificent flight of steps forming the major feature of the east-west axis which links the creek with the off-road car space. Top left, the study window; top right, windows to kitchen/dining and living spaces*

11 *The exciting massing of the building as seen from the car space, at the east end of the east-west axis. In the foreground is the bridge to the front entrance and the route down to the creek*

12 *Looking south, along the north-south axis, to the geometrically sculptural picture gallery and bedroom end of the house*

13 and 14 *South-west window wall to the kitchen/dining space on the ground floor and living space on the first floor. The staircase tower to the viewing deck and the acute plan angle give this corner a theatrical perspective*

15 (overleaf) *From across the creek the lines of the house are softening as the planting extends and grows thicker. Eventually it will be allowed, like a ruin, almost to disappear into its background. The steps to the right of the boathouse are from the west end of the east-west axis*

14

ARCHITECT'S OWN FAMILY RESIDENCE
AT ZURICH-WITIKON

ARCHITECT
Justus Dahinden

JOB ARCHITECT
H. Rüegger of the Dahinden
Office

ENGINEER
E. Sucki and H. Hofacker

The brief which architect Justus Dahinden set himself was straightforward: a five-bedroom house with three bath or shower rooms; a living/dining space containing a sunken area with open fireplace; a breakfast bar to a very well-equipped kitchen with a separate laundry room; a bathroom en-suite with the main bedroom; terraces on different levels and a swimming pool.

The site he found was a treed hillside, sloping down southwards in a low density residential suburb of Zürich, some 15 minutes' car drive from his office in the city centre. By international standards, it is a beautiful situation, although by the standard of Switzerland's own mountain and lake landscape, it is quietly modest.

The house was well built into the hillside, right against the northern boundary, enabling the south-oriented garden in front of the house to cover as large an area as possible. This main garden at ground-floor level has, in fact, been designed as a sun-terrace surround to the large swimming pool, with low maintenance shrub planting restricted to two asbestos cement planters and the hillside to the east of the pool terrace. These plants merge into the trees and shrubs of the higher hillside behind the house and, since the boundary cannot be seen, the house appears set into semi-wild forest. The whole of the southern, built up, part of this terrace is surrounded by a wall of vertically positioned old railway sleepers; these have also been used (although bleached) as a suspended deck around the same end of the pool. The remaining surfaces of the terraces are of washed concrete slabs, including the treads of a splendid multi-terraced flight of steps which links the ground and first-floor main terraces. As this flight rises it shapes itself around a sculptural group of four storey-height vertical cylinders clad in the same roughcast rendered surface as the rest of the house exterior walling (where not glazed), and most of the interior walling. The tops of these cylinders are planted with horizontally spreading thick green plants. The whole composition, with the curving dark copper roof fascias of the first floor projecting behind the cylinders, forms a piece of pure architectural theatre of rare quality.

From the road the house, with its curved south-west corner, appears militarily sturdy and impregnable; this effect is not lessened by the brilliant orange/red painted door to the lower ground-level built-in double garage. The approach to the entrance porch, recessed into the west elevation, is up a wide flight of steps flanked by well-planted slopes. Part of this porch forms a 'tunnel' through to the swimmng pool terrace, to which there are views out from the entrance hall, bedroom and children's

living-room/guest bedroom on this level. Also accommodated here are two bath or shower rooms, a fourth bedroom, boiler room and two 6500 litre oil storage tanks, general storage and the mandatory Swiss underground bomb shelter. With the over-hanging upper terrace, the lighting at this ground level, even with all-white walls and carpet, is quite dramatic. As one ascends the helical staircase to the first floor, a feeling of brightness and openness becomes ever greater until one steps out of the top lit white staircase cylinder into the middle of a glowing white first-floor penthouse, the roughcast rendered walls providing a perfect background for the architect's icon collection. A curving north-west corner wall echoes the staircase tower, the glossy black circular open-hearth fire stand and its hood set in the sunken sitting area, and, ingeniously, a floor-to-ceiling cylinder, also roughcast, which contains the flue from the boiler below and performs the other functions of delineating the open-plan kitchen entrance and the line/length of the breakfast bar

1

the small, but most efficiently planned, detailed and equipped kitchen has views to the dining/living space and out through the fully glazed south-facing wall to the broad, partly roofed and well-landscaped terrace with its splendid views out over the hillsides and down to the blue swimming pool.

The main bedroom continues the internal space, off the dining area; basically still open-plan, it can be closed off by a sliding wall. Off the north end of the bedroom is its bathroom, through which is a laundry room, and here the circulation route is completed with access to the kitchen. These three spaces are all finished robustly in orange tile and dark stained wood.

Construction of the building is brick with roughcast rendering, reinforced concrete floors, and roof with thermal and water insulation, topped with grit and gravel. All internal floors have wall-to-wall deep wool carpeting except for the kitchen, bathroom, etc which have ceramic tiles. The window-walls are black stove-enamelled aluminium frames and panels with Thermopane double-glazed units. Security has been well considered at the design stage with external metal roller blinds housed above the windows. The lighting is mainly Lytespan: spotlights or down lighters, supplemented by a number of free-standing lamps. Doors, divider walls and fitted cupboards are all made of dark stained fir or, in the kitchen, oak. Heating is by hot water radiators and convectors from an oil-fired boiler.

Justus Dahinden is never an architect to take the simplest solution for the planning and design of a new building, although the old boathouse remodelled into his week-end house is, by contrast, just that. Here he has converted his self-brief into a complex but, on study, very practical plan, a plan which has a dramatic built-form, but not too exciting for its environment. Finally, it has the best in Swiss detailing and construction. One cannot, anywhere, expect better than that.

1 *The house from the south-west set into its semi-wild forest landscape. The garage doors are painted a dark orange/red*

2 *From the south-east this view across the swimming pool is a piece of pure architectural drama: the palatial, terraced stair, the huge planted cylinders, the apparently massive cantilevered roof: none of them 'necessary', but together perhaps forming the modern equivalent of the spectacular Italian Renaissance gardens*

3 *The top of the staircase (left) leads out to this white carpeted 'penthouse' with its views out to the terraces and the broad staircase down to the swimming pool. The orange centre plate in the circular open hearth can be removed, revealing a grid for wood burning*

4 *Looking from the main bedroom to the dining area. Between the two massive roughcast cylinders can be seen the breakfast bar, with the sunken sitting area off to the left*

5 *Justus Dahinden house: the beautifully detailed kitchen, seen over the breakfast bar*

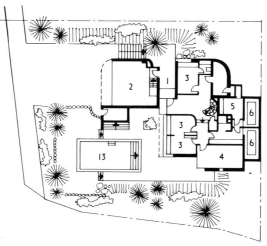

JUSTUS DAHINDEN HOUSE: plans and section

1 entrance
2 garage
3 children's bedrooms
4 guest room/TV room
5 boiler room
6 oil tanks
7 living-room
8 kitchen
9 utility room
10 shower/bathroom
11 main bedroom
12 outdoor terrace
13 swimming pool

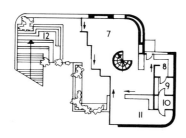

5

6 View through ground-floor entrance hall, past the robust helical staircase to the children's living-room in the centre background. Note how the white finishes and carpet bounce the limited daylight around. With darker finishes this could be a gloomy zone
7 In the main bedroom one is surrounded by texture, soft and hard, contrasted with dark-polished wood. The hanging behind the bed is light orange graduated to brown edges
8 From the terrace, a night view of the first-floor 'penthouse' living space with its sunken sitting area, circular open fireplace and cylindrical hood echoing the roughcast staircase cylinder behind. At the right a glimpse of the dining area

THREE-HOUSE INTERLOCKING GROUP
AT HADDENHAM, BUCKINGHAMSHIRE

ARCHITECT
Peter Aldington of Aldington,
Craig & Collinge

This small group of three houses, known as Turn End, originated from the architect's belief that in villages one ought, where possible, to build houses in groups rather than the all too common 'developer's detached' approach. So, when looking for a site for his own house, he persuaded his family to join him in building a small housing group.

A site was found near the centre of the large Buckinghamshire village of Haddenham, with a population of around 3000, which has, over many centuries, spread in a linear manner for about a mile. It thus had a framework which had been able to cope with something like a 100 per cent increase in size in the preceding ten years without losing its basic character. This character is somewhat unusual in that the village was originally built out of the local clay, called wychert. This was puddled with straw and made into 15 in thick walls, used not only for houses but also to build walls which surround cottage gardens, link houses together and generally provide a unique character and sense of privacy in the many small closes and pedestrian footpaths.

This wall and cottage character was one of the starting points in the design of the present group. Another important factor was that the site's only access was in the south-west corner; so to obtain south and west sunlight and privacy, without losing the tight grouping which was the *raison d'être* for the scheme, it was necessary to adopt a courtyard formation. Privacy was seen as an essential feature from the outset.

The site is bounded on three sides by the original walls and, where possible, these have been used to link the new with the old. It contains a number of very fine trees, which influenced the siting of the houses. The architect's own house is built round a courtyard containing three acacia trees which had been drawn up into a tall slender shape, making them ideal for courtyard use. A basic two-bedroom plan was designed, and this was then modified for each house in turn, according to its position in relation to the others, and its varying function.

One of the over-riding considerations in working out the basic plan was a strong feeling that the kitchen ought to become a true 'living-room' and not a small room facing north at the back of the house, as so often happens. So the kitchen/dining hall is the first room one enters.

In the centre of the house, with all rooms and spaces opening off it, *this* kitchen faces south. A floor-to-ceiling window wall opens fully onto a delightful informally landscaped terrace and pool courtyard, oriented to receive sunlight throughout the day. The living-room, which opens off the kitchen, has a high east window which catches the

morning sun, pouring it right through the house. It also has a glass wall facing west onto the courtyard which can be opened, and this receives late afternoon and evening sunlight.

It was decided to use a material for the walls which required rendering because the wychert walls of the old village are invariably rendered. So the external walls and many of the internal load-bearing walls are constructed out of solid 9 in foamed concrete blocks. The external rendering has a positive function in protecting this blockwork from the weather. The roofs are tiled with Redland Delta tiles in a terracotta colour. This aroused much comment as the colour is initially somewhat bright. However, it was felt that eventually the colour would mellow with moss and algae growth, as it has now done, as have the old corrugated pantiles which are typical of the village, and which were originally equally bright. External timber is creosoted. The carport was deliberately constructed to be reminiscent of local farm lean-to sheds, in the belief that it would acceptably house the cars and be a strong enough form to prevent them dominating the forecourt.

Internally the blockwork is exposed and painted white and the structural roof timbers are all exposed and treated with a clear lacquer. The living area floors are in red quarry tiles with off-peak electric floor heating. The bedroom floors, which are on a raised level, are softwood boarding, sealed, and heating for this area is by a fan assisted electric storage heater centrally placed and ducted into each bedroom. There were three practical reasons for raising the floor of the bedroom area: first to enable the use of high window sills inside, making these even higher outside, for security reasons; secondly to provide a space for service pipes and electric wiring; and thirdly, to help the children with the idea of 'going upstairs to bed'.

As this is another example of a building acclaimed internationally, the fact that it was refused planning permission by Buckinghamshire County Council for 15 months should be recorded. This seems to have been due to an extraordinary, new and quite arbitrary building line drawn on almost all streets in Haddenham, regardless of its environmental effect by the Highways Department, without the agreement of the Planning Department. This line would have cut half way through the first house in the group. The Aldington project was caught up in this internal political wrangle and is proof indeed of the chaos governing UK planning laws and their application by the local authority bureaucracy, bureaucracy which permits 'on the nod' builder development schemes based solely on the amount of financial return and bearing little, if any, considered

1 *Looking from the court to the centrally placed dining/kitchen area. Note the carefully considered and executed timber detailing overall*

relationship to existing village landscape or townscape. Quite clearly from this (and there are many other examples), local authority planning departments are not always capable of recognising sympathetic modern environmental design at the drawing stage.

Although completed in 1967 the group shown here remains outstanding internationally in modern house design. About the only way in which its age is felt, although not shown, is in its insulation: in those days of cheap energy, 1½ in of polystyrene insulation in roof and floor, plus foamed concrete block walling, was good. However, what the house lacks in present-day insulation, it more than makes up for by its wonderfully peaceful, warmhearted and welcoming atmosphere. At night, with its carefully positioned spot lighting, the feeling is, perhaps, closest to that of being in a very sophisticated mountain hut. The subconscious of Peter Aldington, keen hill walker and mountain climber, could well have been aiming for just that.

The passing of time has helped to merge this group into the local vernacular to an even greater degree than when first built and photographed. It has become a place which groups of architects from outside the UK include on their tours, with every justification.

2

2 *View from the living space (built-in seating on the right) to the dining area, with hall and front door (off to the right) in the background*

3 *Crisp and thoughtful detailing in the open, general courtyard, with built-in planter and milk bottle shelf. View to the north from under the farm-like lean-to car port.*

3

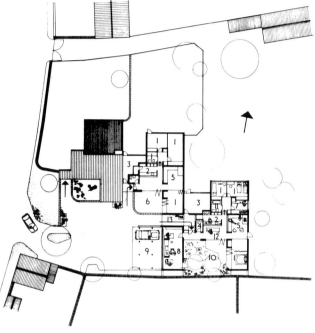

PETER ALDINGTON THREE-HOUSE
GROUP: plan

1 bedroom
2 kitchen
3 storage
4 cloaks
5 living room
6 court
7 dressing room
8 studio
9 car port
10 courtyard
11 bathroom
12 dining room
13 entrance

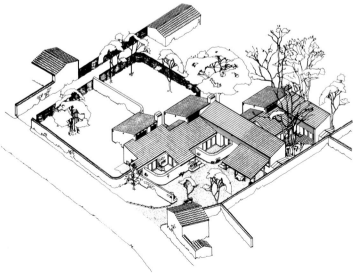

Perspective drawing

4 *The group of three houses seen from the west under a low evening sun. The architect has achieved a gem of vernacular design, yet with a decidedly modern feel to it*

5 *The double-height living space by day. The glazed door to the main garden is at the right. The built-in seating has a classic simplicity and there is timber storage next to hearth*

6 *The same space lit by artificial light, as a contrast to 5. The counter-balanced step ladder leads up to a gallery workroom for the wife of the architect*

FREE-PLAN FOUR-HOUSE GROUP
AT CUSAGO, MILAN

ARCHITECT
Piano + Rogers

PARTNER-IN-CHARGE
Renzo Piano

STRUCTURAL ENGINEER
Flavio Marano

GENERAL CONTRACTOR
CIECI srl, Milan

'Factory houses.' So the architects, with dry humour, introduced this group of four detached dwellings to the author. Only in the sense that there was almost complete spatial freedom for the owners to design their own interiors in the 15 × 12 m open-plan areas, and in the strong exterior visual emphasis placed on roof structure (as might be expected from the architects of the Centre Pompidou) was this description fair.

Given a planning restriction of 25 per cent building area to total site, the basic aim of the architects was to provide at a reasonable cost 180 m² (approx 1600 ft²) of unrestricted internal space, with a storage cellar of the same area. Structurally this has been achieved by building two 15 m long by 4·40 m high brick side walls 15 m apart, and by spanning the space between with eight 1·25 m deep main lattice girders, plus cross and diagonal secondary bracing beams and ties. The structure has not been closed in at the sides. Fixed to the top of this roof structure is a plastic coated ribbed sheet metal covering, to keep the worst of the elements from the structure and the lower roof, the latter suspended at the junctions between main and cross beams underneath the structure.

This lower roof consists, in three of the houses, of a sheet metal sandwich with an inner core of expanded polyurethane; below this, hanging from the same supports, are the ceiling panels. In the fourth, the Lucci house, the roof insulation has been upgraded with a 7 cm glass reinforced polyester/polyurethane/glasswool sandwich. Apart from the reduction in heating costs, this has the further benefit of reducing condensation on the girders above, with a consequent lessening in their maintenance requirement in what is a rather damp region of Europe. Heating of the houses is by individual natural gas boilers with hot water radiators.

The side walls are windowless, and the detail photograph of the creeper on the Simi house shows the beginning of the effect which, it is anticipated, will in a few years' time almost completely hide these walls from view.

In complete contrast the cross walls have a glazed floor-to-ceiling area which is 50 per cent of their total. There is a basic 1·5 m module to these walls, with alternating solid 'Glasol' (asbestos cement backed with polyurethane) panels and fixed- or full-height sliding glazing. On some of the houses, an occasional 3 m solid or fixed-glazed panel creates subtle and pleasant variations in the rhythms of the otherwise identical looking façades.

The setting back of these walls 1·5 or 2 m from the leading edges of the roof keeps the sun off the glazing during the hottest part of the day/year and has provided long dual terraces for each house. Oriented north/west and south-east, these terraces satisfy requirements for sunbathing or cool relaxation at different times of the day and seasons of the year.

Ventilation is provided by inward opening fanlights when the glazed sliding door panels are closed.

Security, an aspect not often given special attention at the design stage of private houses, has been carefully considered here. Every glazed panel in these walls has its own external steel-framed sliding shutter which can be slid across in seconds and rigidly fixed into position, whenever necessary. The shutters visually form an exact match with the solid panels in the walls, and when partly open, partly closed form another strong visual variable in the elevations.

Internally the houses were each contracted to have twin bath/shower/WC rooms. Only minor variation in the size and position of these was possible (although all six, as shown on the plans, have quite different equipment layouts), and the position of the smaller spaces related to these service rooms was therefore in some measure predetermined. All four houses have made use of the large span roof to create the most spacious open-plan entrance/hall/living/dining/kitchen, or in one case photographic studio, which their other requirements allow. The three houses which are being considered have also all divided their smaller spaces with full-height storage walls. So much for the similarities between the houses.

Roberto and Simonetta Lucci, industrial designer and illustrator/teacher respectively, needed a large studio and library. They decided to position this room right across one end of the house, siting the twin bathroom core further into the main space than in the other two houses. Their own individual sitting areas were placed at each end of the space near the floor-to-ceiling glazing, and separated by low level storage and a high drafting-enlarger cubicle. This studio requirement resulted in a long L-shaped main living space which has been immaculately detailed and laid out, one feels in the only possible, the ideal, arrangement. The all-white walls and ceiling with subtly coloured furnishings and carpeting, and with small bright movable colour accents, give a feeling here and throughout the house of soft glowing brightness, and a calmness, almost ecclesiastical, which is at the same time stimulating. The furniture, light fittings and storage walls are designed by Lucci's own firm, L/O Design.

Cesare Simi, lawyer, and his wife Paola who is studying at a Milan school of interior architecture

also needed a small studio in their house, but chose to make use of the basement for this. They have combined it with a hobby room and next door have made a children's playroom for their two young children.

Consequently even more main space than in the Lucci house was available at ground-floor level. Here the plan form is a chunky L, for formal dining, informal dining, kitchen, a breakfast bar and a sitting area, in which experimental changes of furniture position and planter layout can be, and are, made: the plan illustrated shows a different layout from the space as photographed. High contrast and strong colour tone in this house produce visual excitement and drama; with the dark polished tile floor the feeling is that here one must be in Italy. Again, beautiful detailing and finishes in the storage walls and kitchen fitments.

Very different from the two interiors so far covered is that in the house of architect Dr Stefania Gianotti, who designed it, and her husband Annibale Pepe, communications consultant. The storage wall in the main space and studio are faced with high contrast dynamic ballet action photo-murals, but despite this the general attention is caught here by the mass of greenery: is this, one asks, a treed arbour roofed over, or perhaps a summerhouse which has been allowed, deliberately, to become part of the nature surrounding it. This feeling is most emphasised by

the architect in the centrally projecting kitchen, which is hung with several dozen tradescantia plants on chain-suspended shelves and work tops, together with bamboo plants growing up from floor planters, to the extent of almost hiding it from view. A marvellous translucent screen to prepare meals behind, but at the same time to look through and be a part of this living space. From outside, a delightful way to hide inevitable clutter. The massive dining table, also designed by Stefania Gianotti, has its structure of solid maple, and is topped with a slab of polished Sienite stone.

From the main space one has glimpses through the sliding photo-mural covered doors along both sides of the length of this house into smaller spaces, and through the elegant black perforated screen to the studio. With the green of the planting, the muted greys of the rough cut slate slabs and white tile strips forming the floor and fronts of the built-in kitchen island units, the bright yellow of the external steel-work and window/wall frames and the stark black/white tones of the photo-murals, the overall effect is both mysterious and theatrical; but also, as in a garden, it is peaceful.

What these three design-conscious families have done with the spatial freedom provided by Renzo Piano confirms the advantages of flexible spaces and makes one hope that more 'factory houses' may be built.

1 *View of the four-house group seen in its flat Milanese landscape, from the agricultural land to the east*

2 (overleaf) *The south-facing main garden elevation of the Lucci house, with the sliding steel framed security panels open. The Simi house is in the right background*

3

6

4

5

7

8

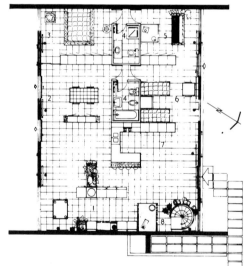

SIMI HOUSE: plan
1 living area
2 dining area
3 master bedroom
4 bathroom
5 TV room
6 children's bedroom
7 kitchen
8 stairs

3 *Lucci house: the kitchen, with the dining space beyond. Note the immaculate detailing, with mirror tiles increasing the feeling of space*

4 *Lucci house: living space, viewed from the storage wall end. The light-diffusing curtains (throughout the house) are fixed in width and are attached to battens which themselves slide on a track at ceiling level*

5 *Lucci house: the bedroom, with a glimpse of the bathroom at the left. The cupboard storage wall backs onto the studio storage wall*

6 *Lucci house: the double studio with Simonetta Lucci, who is an illustrator and Roberto Lucci, an industrial designer*

7 *Simi house: the kitchen with its breakfast bar and deep-gloss cupboard storage wall behind. The formal dining area is in the left background*

8 *Simi house: view over the breakfast bar to the living space*

9

10

11

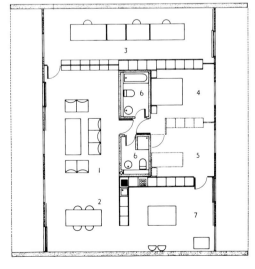

9 *Simi house: part of the south elevation to the main garden. This was the first garden of the four to be planted*

10 *Simi house: the shower room, with its mirror end wall and dramatic lighting*

11 *Gianotti house: looking along the south terrace and, inside, towards the*

screen and beyond it, Stefania Gianotti's studio space. Part of the kitchen can be seen to the right. Note also the detail of the sliding inner glazed and outer steel security doors

12 *Gianotti house: looking from the dining to the living space. The kitchen is to the right. The pictures on the wall are cleverly and simply suspended from an aluminium curtain track*

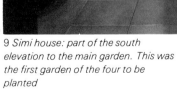

LUCCI HOUSE: plan

1 living area
2 dining area
3 study/work area
4 bedroom
5 spare bedroom
6 bathroom
7 kitchen

12

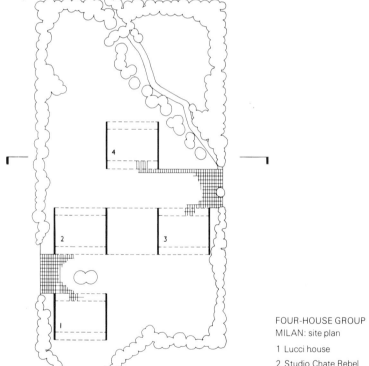

FOUR-HOUSE GROUP
MILAN: site plan

1 Lucci house

2 Studio Chate Rebel

3 Simi house

4 Gionnotti house

Section through short dimension

Section lengthwise

COURTYARD FARMHOUSE
IN AN ORCHARD, BUCKINGHAMSHIRE

ARCHITECT
Arup Associates

PARTNER-IN-CHARGE
Peter Foggo

This is a house of a little under 200 m². beautifully sited in a Buckinghamshire apple orchard of about 3½ ha. The owner is a company executive with a keen interest in part-time farming, and his wife enjoys running the small fruit and free-range poultry farm, of about 8 ha, which surrounds the house. There are three children.

The house was designed about an internal courtyard, landscaped by the owners, around which there are four wings. The first, as one approaches through the apple trees, contains the main entrance, utility, WC and storage rooms. On the right of this is the living wing, containing open-plan kitchen, dining and sitting space which extends out onto a spacious south-west oriented terrace, through floor-to-ceiling glazing. The pictures show the interesting furnishing by Rosenthal. On the left of the main entrance is a wing containing a farm office/spare bed-sitter, plus three children's bedrooms well separated from the third wing on the opposite side of the courtyard which contains the master bedroom suite and a formal entertaining room. The second and third wings form a partial enclosure for the swimming pool and its terrace.

The house is simply constructed from load-bearing brickwork and timber, although the main roof gutter detailing, combined with paired doussie sprocket eave overhangs, gives a welcome visual complexity to the facades. The roof covering is blue-black asbestos cement slates and lead, fixed on battens, counter battens, heavy duty polythene, 25 mm fibreglass quilt, and 25 mm polyurethane foam pre-bonded to plasterboard.

Particular consideration has been given by the architects to the heating of the house and pool by three different sources:

● Two specially designed wood-burning stoves have been installed, one in the main living area and one in the entertaining room, mainly to take advantage of the readily available timber from the surrounding apple orchard.

● A fairly standard hot water radiator system served by an oil-fired boiler in the utility room provides full heating to the house with the majority of radiators having thermostatic valves fitted for automatic temperature control. This system also provides heat to an indirect hot water cylinder in the conventional way, except that the heat exchanger in the cylinder is much larger than normal to allow a full 30 gallons of domestic water to be fully heated in 15 minutes.

● Solar panels covering the south-facing aspect of one complete roof area provide heat when available to the domestic hot water cylinders and the swimming pool. The pool has no other form of heating although the solar heating system has been designed to give priority to the hot water cylinders. The operation, which is fully automatic through a system of controls, is such that whenever solar heating is available, water will pass from the panels to a pre-heating hot water cylinder mounted below the main hot water cylinder. This water will pass through a heat exchanger in the lower cylinder and heat the domestic water to the desired temperature. When this limit is reached the solar water will be diverted to the swimming pool heat exchanger and continue to warm the pool. If the domestic hot water temperature is not reached by solar heating due to weather conditions, the oil-fired boiler plant will automatically 'top-up' the domestic hot water temperature. However, in order to take the best possible advantage of available solar heat, the boiler topping-up process is held off for as long as possible, which is the reason for having an oversized heat exchanger in the main hot water cylinder.

As is often found with courtyard houses, this one too enjoys a soft and very pleasant brightness in its daylighting, which penetrates to unexpected places. This atmosphere is enhanced by the open structure roofs which all have fully glazed end gables, and by the sparkle of water in the court.

The architects have created a modern farmhouse with the friendly open ambiance of an old one. It is well suited to the active life of the family who commissioned it.

1 *The impressive main entrance in the north elevation. Through the glazed entrance screen the internal court can be seen*

2 (overleaf) *Low evening sun on north-facing main entrance elevation*

3 *The house seen from a telescopic pole in its orchard setting in a view from the south-west. Note the solar heating panels in the far roof*

4 *Looking from the west into the dining-room, with the kitchen beyond*

5 *Typical detail at the roof/gutter/wall junction*

6 *The swimming pool and south-east corner of the children's bedroom wing. The solar heating panels can be seen in the roof*

7 *Late summer view of the south-west terrace in the early evening, looking into the living/dining room*

3

4

6

8 *The internal garden court, looking north towards the main entrance, from the entertaining room*

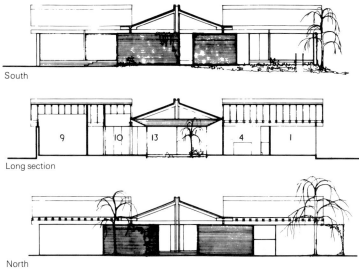

South

Long section

North

COURTYARD FARMHOUSE,
BUCKINGHAMSHIRE: sections
Ground floor plan

1 living area	7 dressing room
2 dining area	8 storage
3 TV area	9 bedroom
4 kitchen	10 office
5 entertaining area	11 utility room
6 bathroom	12 WC
	13 courtyard
	14 bicycle storage
	15 swimming pool

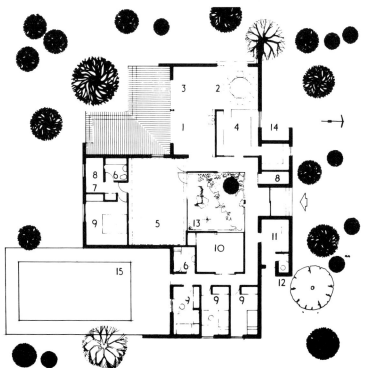

FARMER'S SOLAR HEATED HOUSE
AT FLUY, PICARDY

ARCHITECT-DESIGNER
Ian Ritchie and Jocelyne van den Bossche of Chrysalis Architects

LANDSCAPE DESIGN
Robin Ritchie and Julie Waugh Ritchie Chetham Partnership

STRUCTURAL CONCEPT
Anthony Hunt, Anthony Hunt Associates

Picardy is famous architecturally for its cathedrals, of which it has seven, including Beauvais and Amiens. In total contrast, near the latter city the province now has, tucked away in the rolling countryside, miles from the nearest main road, a small piece of the most elegant, modern and technically up-to-the-minute architecture to be seen anywhere in the world. The location for this building is the little village of Fluy, and the client was neither a jet-setter nor an architect: he was a successful local pig farmer approaching retirement age who, with his wife, wished to hand over their farmhouse to the next generation of the family.

The site available was not exciting: a fenced-off part of a flat pig field, close to the old farmhouse. As architect, a family friend, Ian Ritchie (who has worked with Norman Foster, and in West Germany and Japan) was chosen, together with designer and photographer Jocelyne van den Bossche, daughter of the client.

The requirements of the client — whose experience of house types was limited to traditional and 'catalogue standard houses' (which dominate the French private housing market) — were developed during the course of discussions, as follows. The house was to be practical and with low maintenance; it was to have very large storage facilities; a dining space to accommodate family reunions of up to 30 people; a grandchildren's play space separate from their bedroom; a traditional wine cellar; an enclosed garage with simple access to the house. An idea for large areas of glass, the better to appreciate a garden, developed into the concept of 'living in a garden under a well-insulated umbrella'.

Since the garden was to be a fundamental part of the whole design, the architectural and landscaping teams worked together from the beginning to create an integrated environment.

Ian Ritchie and Jocelyne van den Bossche knew that not only were they going to design this building, they were also going to build it. Therefore all details were to be kept simple.

A design concept was worked out by the architect:

● to develop a modular construction kit which could be assembled by unskilled labour and which would be adjusted to suit the particular needs of the client during final stages of assembly.
● to build as much space as possible to high standards within the budget.
● to provide all-round visual awareness of external spaces by starting with all four sides of the house in glass to which could be added privacy screens and solar panels on a modular basis once the client became acclimatised to the house and could partici-

pate in final arrangements.
● to construct a hole in the ground by exploiting the natural angle of repose of the clay subsoil, thus eliminating the need for retaining walls and tanking to provide wine storage and solar energy storage areas; to use the excavated soil for landscaping.
● to exploit solar energy, if possible, and particularly to ensure that the house would consume less energy than a traditional house of comparative volume, despite the high percentage area of glass cladding.

A construction kit was, accordingly, designed and a manufacturer in Eire found, able to deliver to the site the complete package consisting of steel frame, external cladding elements, roof panels, insulation, ceiling panels, solar collector panels, internal partitions and flooring panels. The cost of this, delivered, came to £50/m².

With the exception of excavations and concrete, the heating, electrical and sanitary installation which were sub-contracted locally, and the roof waterproofing which was sub-contracted in the UK, the house was constructed entirely by the architect-designer team of two in ten months. This included complete erection of the construction kit, finishing of the services installations, fabrication and finishing of all built-in furniture, beds, workbenches, play equipment and removal service; with more experience, they say, the time could well have been reduced to seven months.

The landscaping, designed to provide wind-breaks as well as visual interest and privacy in the flat surroundings, took, with limited equipment, four people three months to complete. The bankings were built up from the house cellar excavations, and the garden was in the main complete before the house which helped the client to a better understanding of the 'living in a garden' concept.

In achieving the aims of low heating energy use, which are particularly important today, the following factors were applied in the design: orientation of the house to maximise solar heat gain; planning of interior spaces to respond to occupancy periods and sun movement; a high level of thermal insulation, the roof; low internal height to give minimum house volume; landscaping to provide wind-breaks; services void beneath the house to provide a stable below-floor temperature; and lastly, absorption of freezer, fridge and lighting energy into the heat distribution system.

The house has an oil-fired heating installation into which the solar energy heating is fed. The integration occurs in three ways:

● sunrays are allowed to hit the floor (dark grey) within the house via the fully glazed south face. The

nergy is trapped passively.

sunrays in the morning and evening, when they
re at low angle, are allowed to hit the vertical solar
ollector panels on the east and west faces. This
nergy, moving by natural convection and assisted
y a central fan, enters the house through manually
perated ventilators before being directly redis-
ibuted or stored.

sunrays between 10.00 and 15.00 hours are
lowed to hit the garden solar collector. This
ollector acts as a 24 hours storage facility as well as
rewarming the fresh air supply to the house.

All the solar energy captured is transferred by air,
nd the solar energy installation is directed only to
pace heating.

The house heated volume is 500 m³ and the
stimated fuel consumption based on the first two
inters of occupation 1977-8 and 1978-9 is
500-3000 litres per annum, maintaining a day
emperature of 20-21°C and a night temperature of
6°C. Compared to traditional houses in the area (10
res per m³ heated space per annum), this indicates
cost saving on space heating of 40 per cent.

The total capital investment in solar energy
aterials was £700 which included the twin use of
e vertical solar collectors as insulating walls and
nergy captors, the garden solar collector, ventila-
rs and electronic temperature sensor. This means

that the investment should be recuperated after
three heating seasons.

There seem to have been two types of local
reactions to this house. The first is by those who,
though finding the outside of the house a mystery in
relation to the traditional buildings of the village,
nevertheless accept it because of the related landscaping. The second is by people with professional
occupations who, in addition to appreciating the
house/garden relationship, are also able to
comprehend intellectually this logical use of
contemporary materials and technology.

Considering their background and age, the clients
had some radical decisions to make during this
project. But they moved into the new home without
any problems, and affirm, giving great satisfaction to
the architect/designer team, that they would now
find it impossible to return to living in a traditional
house.

The concept of 'living in a garden under a well-
insulated umbrella' has been turned into a reality of
building technology with this project. It demon-
strates that the enjoyment of living in the outside/
inside architectural environment originated by Mies
van der Rohe and Philip Johnson with the Glass
House in 1949 and the Farnsworth House in 1951 is
now open to a very much wider public.

1 *View of the open-plan sitting area
from the entrance hall doorway. Note
the chimney to the open fireplace
penetrating the glazing*

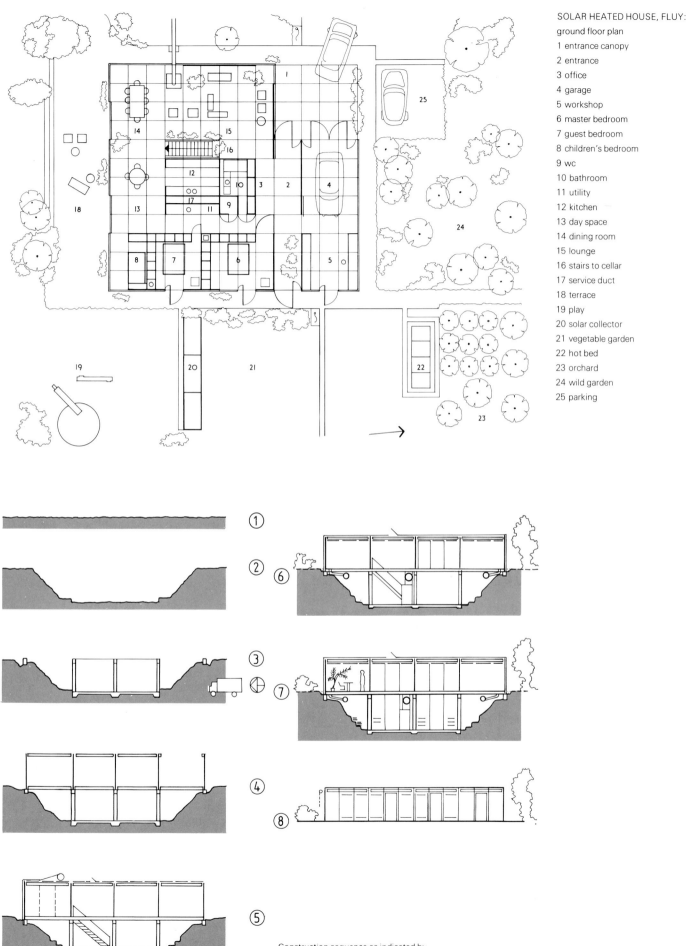

SOLAR HEATED HOUSE, FLUY:
ground floor plan
1 entrance canopy
2 entrance
3 office
4 garage
5 workshop
6 master bedroom
7 guest bedroom
8 children's bedroom
9 wc
10 bathroom
11 utility
12 kitchen
13 day space
14 dining room
15 lounge
16 stairs to cellar
17 service duct
18 terrace
19 play
20 solar collector
21 vegetable garden
22 hot bed
23 orchard
24 wild garden
25 parking

Construction sequence as indicated by
numbers

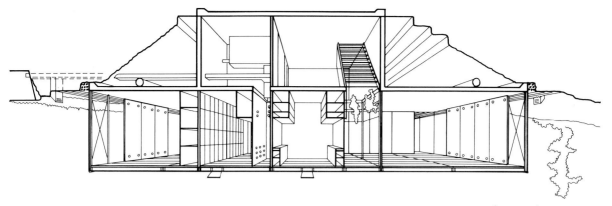

Axonometric

Cellar plan
1 playroom
2 storage
3 heating
4 access
5 wine cellar
6 vegetable storage
7 solar storage zone
8 heating unit

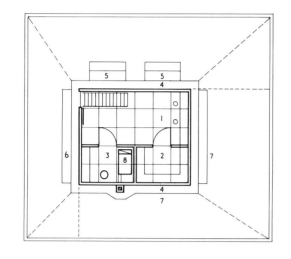

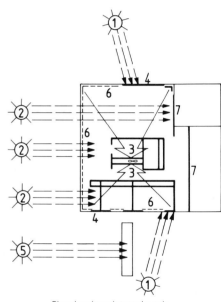

Plan showing winter solar gain

Diagrams illustrating solar heat gain and loss

1 sunrays hitting solar panels
2 sunrays directly into house
3 heat 'pulled' to redistribution duct
4 solar panels
5 sunrays hitting garden collector

6 insulating curtain
7 insulating wall
8 insulating roof
9 energy storage
10 wind effect reduced by landscape

11 heating/recycling plant
12 summer heat allowed to escape
13 summer reflective blinds
14 cross ventilation using rooflights

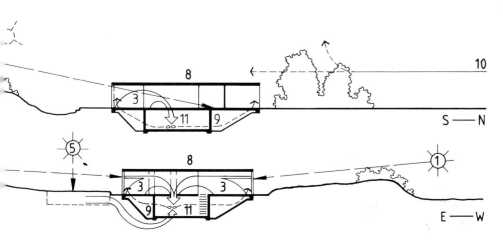

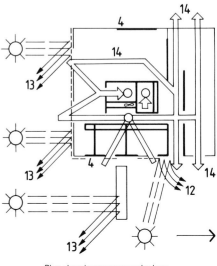

Plan showing summer solar loss

2

3

2 *Tanking of the cellar walls has been avoided by exploiting the natural angle of repose of the subsoil, shown here with its bonus use as a natural wine cellar.*

3 *Detail at the base of the building showing the glazing finishing at ground level, the tensioned guide wires for the exterior solar control blinds, and the fixing for the internal structural tie rod at the base of the column*

4 *Looking over the marble-topped dining table into the well-organised open kitchen*

5 *Looking over the slopes of the landscaped garden to the south façade of the building. In the near background is the old farmhouse*

6 *The elegantly structured house seen in its garden setting, from the south-west*

7 *View to the transparent south-west corner with its dramatically sculptural fabrication of aluminium chimney, TV aerial and dual-role support-structure. In the ground to the left of this structure is a ventilation funnel from the wine cellar*

8 (overleaf) *The south-east corner of the house in its rural setting, seen over the beautifully landscaped garden which formed a part of the same flat pig field. Note the bank of solar collectors*

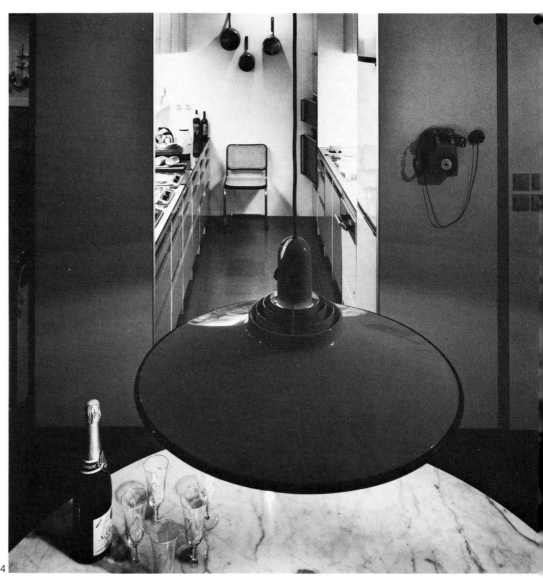

4

7

ARCHITECT'S OWN ENERGY-CONSERVING HOUSE

IN SUSSEX

ARCHITECT
Peter Lambert Gibbs

Architect Lambert Gibbs had been thinking about his ideal family house for at least ten years when he purchased a forester's cottage, unused for 35 years, with two acres of lightly wooded western sloping hillside, some 400 ft up in Ashdown Forest. So, having quickly arrived at the design solution for this site, which he has no hesitation in attributing to the influence of Frank Lloyd Wright, it was a mere seven weeks before his drawings were completed, put before the local authority and planning consent received for a house to replace the existing cottage.

The house was for his family of seven, with five children aged one to eleven. The brief to himself was to provide as much space as possible; flexibility for the changing needs of the growing family; simple internal finishes; sun in all rooms at some time of the day; no external maintenance; some acoustic separation between the parents' and children's parts of the house; a very high standard of thermal insulation to counteract the heat loss through the large areas of external wall and floor which his design concept called for.

Directly employing local bricklayers and carpenters by the hour, Lambert Gibbs supervised the construction himself. This was more expensive than a competitive tender contract, he believes, but it resulted in top quality workmanship.

As can be imagined, after 35 years the site had gone completely wild. Trees had to be cut down, not only to locate the new house, but also to open up a view from it and to let in sunlight. Felling was, however, very carefully considered, and groups of trees were left which form an important and related aspect of the design and positioning of the building.

The structure of the house consists of stone-faced cavity walls with a 9 in or 4½ in brick inner skin, which support, above ground-floor level, an entirely timber-framed structure. The squared stone came from a demolished local barn and Sussex brick from a demolished cottage on the site was used for door and window openings in the stone walls. The main timber beams of the upper structure are 16 × 18 in × 40 ft long; unable to locate a supplier in the UK,

they had to be imported as log from Canada. The upper external cladding is 10 × 1¼ in horizontally jointed cedar boarding with machined edges, and the original mill-sawn finish remaining as the visible face. Fixing is with aluminium nails. The windows and glazed doors to the cantilevered balcony/terraces are heavy section purpose-made wrought cedar to take factory sealed double-glazing units. As is normal, the external cedar is left untreated to weather silver grey, internally, treatment is a clear polyurethane seal.

So much off the beaten track is this house that all its electricity has to be self-generated by a 6kW diesel generator built into the cellar of the old cottage some yards away, and water must be pumped up from a spring at the bottom of the site. Automatic equipment is used for both services.

The most interesting technical feature of this house is undoubtedly the thermal insulation. This is therefore well detailed as follows: the floors have under 1 in t+g boarding: building paper with foil backing, ½ in insulation board; 2 in glass fibre or under the living-room, 7 in of vermiculite; ⅜ in foil backed plasterboard, or ½ in matchboarding on foil backed building paper. The walls behind the external cedar boarding: building paper with foil backing; 4 in glass fibre; ⅜ in foil-backed plasterboard; two coats of vermiculite insulating plaster. The roofs: three layers of glass-fibre based roofing felt plus one of asbestos based felt, all bonded with hot bitumen 2 in of Stramit compressed straw slabs; 4 in of glass fibre; ⅜ in foil-backed plasterboard; two coats of vermiculite insulating plaster. The net result is that this large house can be kept warm using only two radiators, two heated towel rails and the central open log fire which is designed to warm the stone/brick enclosing structure forming a radiator (in the manner of the one-time ubiquitous Continental Dutch tiled stoves) and the Aga cooker in the kitchen. By the standards of insulation used in the UK in the late 1970s, still well short of that in this house completed in 1966, Lambert Gibbs has here produced an energy conserving building ahead of its time by at least 10 years.

1 *Detail of the south corner, showing the mill-sawn finish on the 10 × 1¼ in cedar boarding, seen from the kitchen entrance approach. Window to the entrance hall/dining-room*

2

3

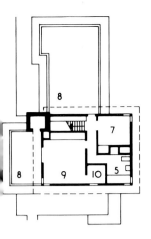

1 entrance hall
2 dining area
3 living room
4 kitchen
5 bathroom
6 wc
7 children's bedrooms
8 terrace
9 parent's bedroom
10 dressing room
11 playroom
12 open storage
13 storage
14 heating

4

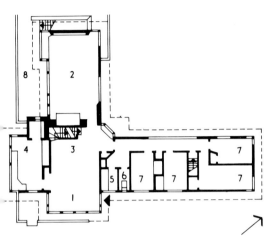

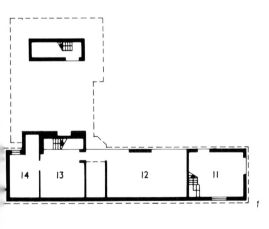

5

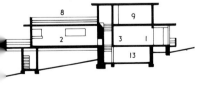

ENERGY-CONSERVING HOUSE IN
SUSSEX:
First floor plan, ground floor plan, lower
ground floor plan, elevation

2 *The living-room with double-glazed doors open to the terrace on the right. The open log fireplace is designed to warm its stone and brick enclosing structure like a Dutch tiled stove*
3 *Looking out from the living-room to the terrace and the slopes of Ashdown Forest*
4 *The simply furnished dining-room/entrance hall, looking out to the south-east*

5 *View up the slope showing the south-west face and the carefully controlled position of the house in relation to the existing trees. The Frank Lloyd Wright influence is clearly seen*
6 (overleaf) *The house, seen from a distance through the trees of Ashdown Forest, projecting from its beautiful hillside location*

GALLERIED APARTMENT REMODELLING

PLACE DES VOSGES, PARIS

ARCHITECT
Richard Rogers + Partners

The Place des Vosges in Paris was built during the years 1605-12. According to Sir Nikolaus Pevsner* it is the best illustration of the French style of brick building with stone quoins and window dressing known as Henri IV.

The northern part of the square is lively, with shops and restaurants under the arcades. It was here in 1976 that architect Richard Rogers was fortunate enough to find a first-floor apartment available. This was just at the time when he needed a Paris base for his massive new building project a few minutes' walk away from the Centre Pompidou.

The contrast between the two concurrent projects must have been highly satisfying: the one, a late 20th-century technological *tour de force* on a grand scale; the other a 17th-century apartment conversion, also in its way (since these are metropolitan city centre houses) on a grand scale.

The original floor-to-ceiling height of the apartment was 4·5 m. At some stage the previous occupants of Rogers's apartment had built an extra floor into this space, completely killing the original splendid conception. It was decided to reinstate and expose the original structure of the building where this had been concealed or neglected by previous conversions.

With the scale of the Centre Pompidou much in mind, thinking in terms of demolishing a floor here was no problem whatever for the architect, and this was done, leaving only a quarter of the main space enclosed as bathroom, utility and boiler room and bedroom, with a large mezzanine gallery bedroom

*An Outline of European Architecture, Pelican, 1943, 7th edn 1963.

over. Access to the latter is by a vivacious tubular steel staircase with perforated metal treads.

The kitchen was built as a freestanding island unit with a post-formed laminate top containing a double sink unit and gas rings. It is truly open-plan with the dining space and the sitting area beyond, one is tempted to say in the distance. For a city centre kitchen, the views this one enjoys, both inside and out, to the quiet architecture and the activity of the treed square, are quite outstanding. It could be thought that with a kitchen completely open to view the normal clutter of cooking would be objectionable, but the scale of this room is so big that it is not, in fact, noticed to such a degree. Behind the kitchen is a further bedroom with access through two sliding doors that are almost floor-to-ceiling either side of the kitchen island unit. These doors increase still further the feeling of openness in the apartment during the day.

White paint, eggshell or cellulose, has been used for the walls and fittings respectively. The floors have sealed terracotta tiles throughout, which look and feel as though they are the original floor but are not. The original timber ceiling beams were cleaned and stained.

A space and situation which must be at least as beautiful and colourful with its art and furnishing now as when built about 370 years ago. With its efficiently organised 20th-century living equipment (including heating by hot-water finned tube set in a continuous floor trench, covered with a neat flush aluminium grill), it must be very much more comfortable and warmer in the winter.

1 *View northwards from the centre group of trees, across the Place des Vosges to the 17th-century housing, with the Rogers's apartment immediately to the left of the central gateway house*

plan
1 living area
2 dining area
3 bedroom
4 kitchen
5 child's bedroom
6 laundry
7 bathroom
8 stairs

2 *Eastward view of the apartment, on the first floor and just to left of centre in this picture, as seen through a corner café window*

3 *Looking towards the courtyard and staircase entrance at the right, with the tempting arcade immediately under the apartment at the left. Sadly the remodelling was not able to include re-routing of mass external wiring*

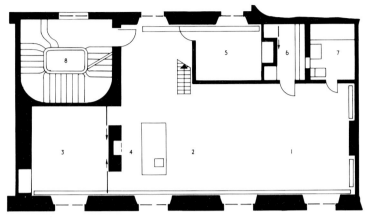

5

6

4 *The huge main living space, 4·5 m high. In the distance the dining area and island kitchen fronted by storage cupboards and with the oven built into the old chimney breast; through the storey-height doorways either side, the main bedroom*

5 *The kitchen with one of the finest metropolitan views anywhere, out over the mellow square with its trees, surrounded by Henri IV-style architecture*

6 *Detail of the staircase to the gallery bedroom, with its structure of welded steel and its treads of heavy gauge perforated aluminium*

HOUSE AMID VICTORIAN GRAND RUINS

IN KENT

ARCHITECT
Michael Manser Associates

ARCHITECTS-IN-CHARGE
Michael Manser, P. Turnbull

ASSISTANT
T. Miller

LANDSCAPE ARCHITECT
B. St. J. Gruffydd

STRUCTURAL ENGINEER
Hockley and Dawson

Company director John Howard, one-time Member of Parliament and PPS to Edward Heath, and his wife were hunting for an out of the ordinary site in Sussex or Kent. They wished to build a small modern labour-saving house which could be used either for weekend or for permanent living.

What they were fortunate enough to find on the market was a two and a half acre site in the Kent hills which contained the ruins and rubble of a large flamboyant Victorian mansion which had been all but totally demolished shortly after the war. It had been built by a millionaire textile manufacturer as the centre piece of his extensive estates, and the chosen position was superb, with splendid views to east, south and west out over the hills and to the hilltop town of Goudhurst.

Previous prospective purchasers of this site had apparently been scared off by the mass of rubble, but the Howards were advised by their architect, Michael Manser, that this was only a very minor problem, and they decided accordingly that here was the place for their house.

The site, after the removal of the rubble, was on two basic levels: an upper terrace, and a lower terrace on the same level as the cellar. All that remained sound of the mansion were the foundations, an ornate stone balustrade to the upper terrace and a grand flight of steps from one terrace level to the other. There was also the shell of the original winter garden, which it was decided would make a fine position for a swimming pool. The flat plateau of the site was backed by forest trees and tiered banks of rhododendron bushes.

In his design Michael Manser has taken the imposing axialities of the staircase linking the terraces, and the centre-line of the winter garden swimming pool as the basis for the positioning of the house. Assisted by his client's wish for large areas of glazing to take in both the distant views and local landscape, he decided to make the house visually as unobtrusive and simple as possible.

To this end, an exposed steel frame main roof structure, on eight rectangular section steel columns, was carefully designed. It has allowed an elegantly thin substructure of timber spanning between steel purlins, insulated with woodwool slabs and finished with bituminous roofing felt.

Since the 16 in main support beams are set well back from the long faces of the building, the roof appears to float out over the aluminium-framed bronze tinted fully glazed walls which, with sliding sections at intervals, are continuous on all four façades. Only on the two short faces is the main supporting structure visible externally and with it a greater feeling of strength. The underside of the roof is faced with Ramin tongued and grooved boarding set between the steel purlins and flush with their soffits.

The internal walls are of dark brown facing bricks and the floors are of dark blue quarry tiles or of white carpeting set into the concrete podium under which is the original cellar. This cellar is used mainly for storage and as a boiler room for the ducted warm air heating system.

The house is approached from the east, and is completely hidden from view by a screen wall until quite suddenly, there before one is this immaculate steel and bronze glass pavilion set in a perfect English lawn with the open view out over the trees to the hills beyond it. From this position the north wall to the winter garden conceals the swimming pool but, approaching the house, this too further surprises the eye with a sparkle of blue water.

Inside, the little entrance lobby leads into the large living space with its peaceful sunken sitting area and open hearth; opening off this at the south-east corner of the house is the dining-room/kitchen. The latter is beautifully detailed with an island hob stainless-steel worktop storage unit as a key feature; above this is a striking cylindrical extract-fan housing. A very far cry from the gloomy Victorian servants' kitchen and all its ancillary accommodation which it replaces with such simple and satisfying panache.

1 *The swimming pool set amid the columns of the old winter garden. Looking from the master bedroom.*

2

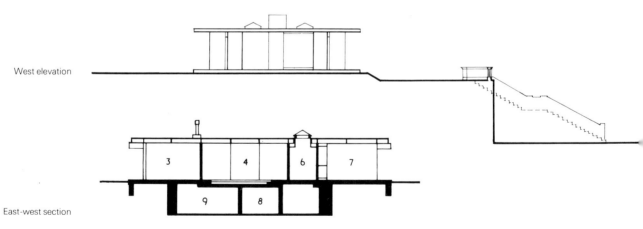

West elevation

East-west section

| 3 | 4 | 6 | 7 |

| 9 | 8 |

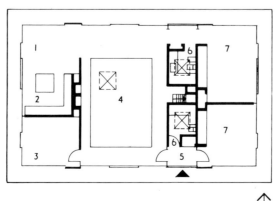

HOUSE AMID VICTORIAN RUINS IN
KENT:
Plan
1 dining area
2 kitchen
3 study
4 living
5 entrance hall
6 bathrooms
7 bedrooms
8 oil store
9 storage

4

2 *View from the master bedroom suite along the south side of the house. To the left, the sunken sitting area; ahead the dining/kitchen area. A major part of the roof structure is exposed in this house, hence the main roof is thinner and lighter-looking than the roofs of the Farnsworth and Glass Houses which influenced this design*

3 *The Victorian flight of steps 'designed to be impressive', leading from the lower terrace up to the house*

4 *A glimpse of the smoothly detailed house, through the robust Victorian winter garden columns*

5 *The dining/kitchen area with its island hob unit and striking cylindrical fibre glass extract-fan housing. Much more efficient and, no doubt, a tenth of the size of the Victorian kitchen complex it replaced*

6 (overleaf) *The house on its grand arcaded podium, delicately echoing the rhythm of the heavier winter garden columns*

REMODELLING OF ARCHITECT'S 19-TH CENTURY STUDIO HOUSE IN LONDON

ARCHITECT
Stephen LeRoith

Stratford Studios consist of six studios grouped along a private access avenue in Kensington. They were built during the middle part of the 19th century, and were originally constructed for the use of successful Victorian artists. Later the studios were taken over by the London School of Art, run by John Hassall (well known for *Skegness is so Bracing*) who was the originator of the correspondence course as a method of teaching art. Thereafter the studios were split up, as they are now, and used for a variety of purposes, including the then young Boyd Neel Orchestra, a boat builder, a firm of architects and an artist in stained glass.

No 3 (illustrated here) has a main working space which is 20 ft wide and 40 ft long and has a ceiling 17 ft high. The roof is supported by two masonry bearing walls at each end, and two intermediate trusses at 13 ft intervals. It is a form of mansard with the slope on the north side entirely glazed to provide natural diffused light at a high level: an ideal source of light for artists.

The purpose of the original design was to provide a suitable working space for artists, with occasional sleeping and cooking facilities. The main space was used entirely as a work area, and the mezzanine gallery was a completely enclosed bedroom. A small kitchen recess was provided in the area which is now the water garden court. A living-room was situated off the kitchen area, which has now been converted to bedroom 2 with its adjoining bathroom.

Although wishing to retain the studio partly as a working space, the architect, Stephen LeRoith, decided to remodel the major part to provide a permanent home for himself and his wife.

The basic concept was to preserve the spatial quality of the studio and to enhance this quality wherever possible. The decision was made, therefore, to retain the main studio space in its open-plan form, the only fixed element being the kitchen recess. The remaining space would contain free-standing furniture, providing living, dining and working areas which are entirely interchangeable according to current needs. The position for bedroom 1 has been retained on the opened-up gallery, with a dressing-room and bathroom neatly adjoining.

The idea of the water garden court arose partly from the need to provide light in bedroom 2 and partly from the overall concept which involved linking the exterior and interior spaces. The court is 8 × 10 ft and the water level is 4 in deep. This is sufficient to grow a wide variety of marginal water plants in wicker baskets. The pool is self-cleaning; a weir has been provided which allows either fresh or rain water to enter the pool, raising the water level and thereby allowing the surface water to run over the weir which strains off the scum and leaves. The pool is cleared once a year through a separate outlet situated in the bottom of the pool. Algae is controlled by means of a chemical additive.

To reduce the cost of the joinery, all the fittings were designed as a simple framework constructed in oak with oak-veneered panels attached. All panels were cut to identical widths, then fixed with hinges to the framework with ¾ in reveals between the panels. The joinery is finished with mat polyurethane. The entire kitchen recess is lined with white formica for easy maintenance.

The heating system has been completely redesigned, with two hot air ducted units, one sited in the cellar under the water garden court, the other under the staircase leading to bedroom 1, providing this service. The units have automatic humidifiers which are housed within the ducts. The heating is divided into two zones, one unit serving the first floor, kitchen and dining recess; the other serving the remainder of the studio. The main studio area is heated from a series of perimeter radiators.

The result of the very carefully executed up-dating exercise is an excellent 20th-century home environment. The studio has become a most spacious and well-lit living hall, which has striking views into it from bedroom 1, and views out from it to the sparkling little water garden court. The reflective qualities of the water and surrounding glazing of this court successfully complement the spatial qualities of this main hall; bedroom 2 and the entrance lobby also have views to the court, which, all in all provides visual pleasure and interest to this home quite out of proportion to its small size.

REMODELLING OF 19TH CENTURY STUDIO HOUSE IN LONDON: plans

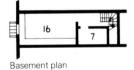

Basement plan

Ground floor plan

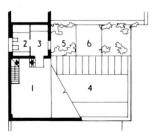

First floor plan

1 main bedroom	9 kitchen recess
2 bathroom	10 living area
3 dressing room	11 bathroom
4 void over living area	12 bedroom 2
5 roof terrace	13 water garden court
6 void over water garden court	14 entrance
7 heating unit and services	15 wc
8 dining area	16 darkroom and storage

1 *View of the the main living hall towards the water garden court, with a soft light from the north-facing glazing*

3

2 (preceding page) *A night view of the thoughtfully lit studio living hall from the dining area. A glimpse of the water garden court at the left*

3 *Looking down into the tiny water garden court with its basket planting*

4 *A general exterior view of No 3 Studio and two of its neighbours as seen from the north-east*

5 *Roofscape view with the water garden court. At the right, the main mansard roof with sloping studio north-light windows*

6 *The finely detailed galley kitchen seen from the dining area*

7 *The main studio living hall, looking towards the gallery bedroom with dining area and kitchen (enclosed) under*

5

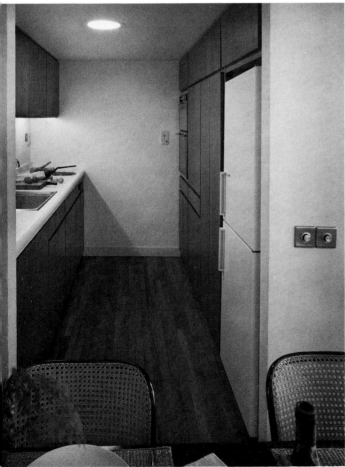

7

ARCHITECT'S OWN HOUSE AND OFFICE

AT STUTTGART

ARCHITECT
Wilfried Beck-Erlang

ASSISTANT
Klaus Schmoller

ASSISTANT INTERIOR DESIGN
Helga Griese

STRUCTURAL ENGINEER
Mr Bauer

HEATING ENGINEER
Mr Laux

ELECTRICAL ENGINEER
Mr Schwarz

LANDSCAPE ARCHITECT
Mr Miller

ENAMEL WORK
Kurt Frank, Painter

Set in among other detached houses of mixed aesthetic value and age, on one of the many hills surrounding the city centre of Stuttgart, the site available for this building could have been daunting: an irregular sided 5000 ft² (5ar) obliquely sloping plot next to a main trunk route, on a 125° corner. The architect, Wilfried Beck-Erlang, with the idea of providing joint living and working space under one roof, wished to design himself a five-bedroom dwelling on this site, plus office/studio accommodation for a staff of about eight.

With confidence and expertise he and his team have created a handsome, sculptural building which, both in plan and section nestling into the hill, has solved the problems involved with an easy flow of eight interconnecting levels and geometrically non-rectangular plan shapes.

The slope has, in fact, been made to assist in the vertical separation of the practice and living areas. The office/studio accommodation is on the lower levels with its own impressive external entrance at street level. The family living levels are above, with main access via a covered external staircase at the side of the double length garage, and with a secondary internal staircase down to the practice off the first-floor entrance hall. At this level is also a guest bedroom and a large 12 ft high parents' living-room/study. Up half-a-level are the main south and west-facing living/dining and kitchen spaces which can be left open or closed off with sliding doors as desired. These spaces look out through floor-to-ceiling fixed or sliding glazing to the main garden, a level area which has been formed from the hill at this plan height.

Surrounded and sheltered by a horizontally board-marked concrete wall, this town garden has been designed to need a minimum of maintenance: pathways of circular stepping stones of exposed small aggregate concrete lead through areas of most carefully graded and positioned large to small loose-laid pebbles, among which are set clumps of springy grass and other infill planting requiring low maintenance. As an extension of the living/dining area inside, an external dining/sitting terrace has been provided on a large rectangle of the same surfaced concrete paving slabs. This terrace is partially open to the sky, partially roofed over by a bridge and extension off the upper terrace (which opens off the main bedroom floor). The terrace is pebbled and planted in the same way as the garden below. It is a casually immaculate garden, the result of much careful thought by the landscape architect Herr Miller; thought, it appears, taken in some ways from the Japanese but here modified for a Western life-style.

At the front of the building, at street level, the garden continues the same theme but here with a smaller proportion of pebbles, and more of the low maintenance planting, bounded by interlocking brick paving.

The main street elevation is clearly designed to express the many differences in plan level. But much of the deep modelling has a practical purpose: the solid concrete-faced balconies and the stepped slab concrete wall at ground level outside the office windows were all designed to reflect traffic noise away from the house. Behind these baffles — and throughout the building — the glazing is either double or triple to provide thermal or high sound insulation. Where the glazing is fixed facing the main road, air-conditioning units under these windows have been built into the walls, which also provide noise-absorbed ventilation. In addition, and for all the other areas of the building not fitted with air conditioning there is heating by an oil-fired boiler at the lowest plan level, serving hot water radiators. General thermal insulation is provided on the 25 cm thick mass concrete walls by 4 cm polystyrene dots and air space behind 1 cm of plasterboard and plaster. This produces a good-looking contrasting finish to the rougher board-marked concrete of the internal walls. In addition there are many carefully detailed cupboard and shelf units of sipo mahogany.

Even more interest is given to the striking exterior appearance of this modelled concrete and glass faced building by the use of external solar control blinds, by a number of royal blue anodised metal panels which give colour accents; and most subtly by balanced variations between different areas of concrete, with either horizontal or vertical board markings. Why balconies on this noisy street front? They serve, in addition to the noise reflector use previously mentioned, primarily as fixed window cleaning platforms. Truly practical sculpture.

1 *View of the house on its corner site, from the north-west. Ahead, the entrance gate, with a covered staircase up to the first-floor entrance to the residence*

2 *The slat concrete wall outside the architect's offices is primarily a traffic noise baffle. View to the north-east on the route to Stuttgart centre*

3 *A part of the south-east elevation showing the balconies which, besides being an integral part of the sculptural effect, act as traffic noise baffles and as window-cleaning platforms*

3

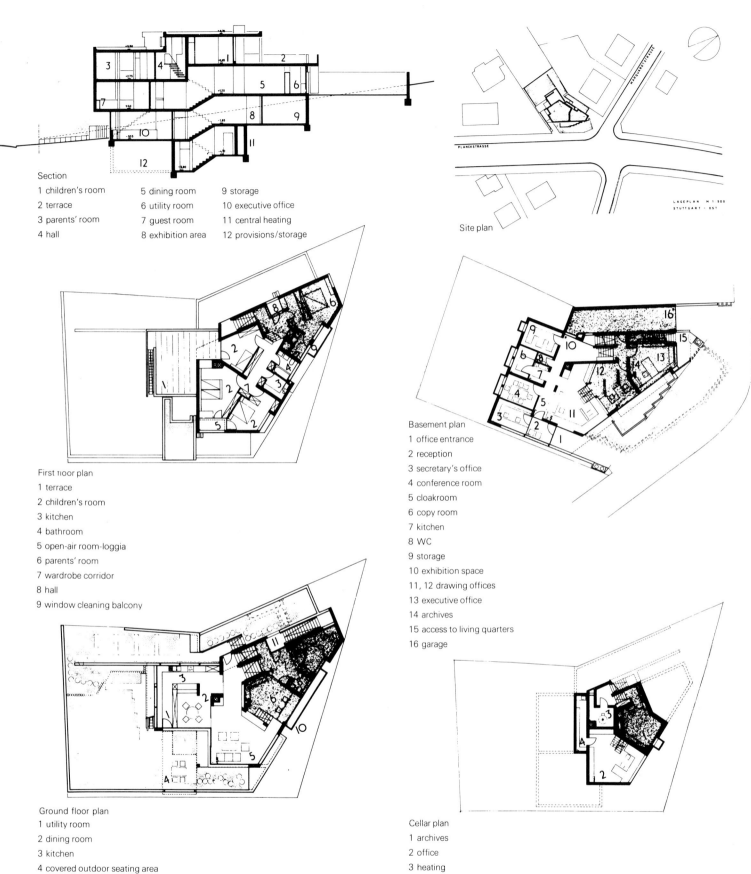

Section

1 children's room
2 terrace
3 parents' room
4 hall

5 dining room
6 utility room
7 guest room
8 exhibition area

9 storage
10 executive office
11 central heating
12 provisions/storage

Site plan

First floor plan

1 terrace
2 children's room
3 kitchen
4 bathroom
5 open-air room-loggia
6 parents' room
7 wardrobe corridor
8 hall
9 window cleaning balcony

Basement plan

1 office entrance
2 reception
3 secretary's office
4 conference room
5 cloakroom
6 copy room
7 kitchen
8 WC
9 storage
10 exhibition space
11, 12 drawing offices
13 executive office
14 archives
15 access to living quarters
16 garage

Ground floor plan

1 utility room
2 dining room
3 kitchen
4 covered outdoor seating area
5 living area
6 study
7 hall
8 WC
9 guest room
10 window cleaning balcony
11 entrance

Cellar plan

1 archives
2 office
3 heating
4 provisions/storage

BECK-ERLANG HOUSE AT STUTTGART

108

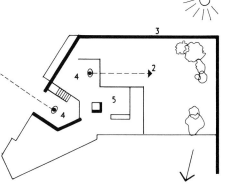

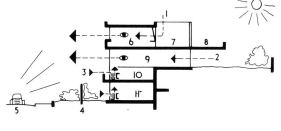

rientation of the living area
here are views east (1) and west (2) into
e garden, and a sound insulating wall (3)
cing the noise zone.

view
view into garden
sound insulating wall
iving area
dining area

Sound insulation and air circulation
There is an air-intake from above via the
loggia (1) and from the garden (2) and via
the sound repellent concrete channel (3).
The sound insulating wall (4) acts as a
buffer against the noise zone (5). The
windows are triple glazed.

1 air intake via loggia
2 air intake via garden

3 air intake via concrete channel
4 sound insulating wall
5 noise zone
6 bedrooms
7 loggia
8 sun terrace
9 upper living area
10 lower living area
11 work/office area

Sound insulation and air-intake of the
bedrooms
There is an air-intake to the bedrooms via
the loggia, which has glazed walls and is
open at the top (1). The bathrooms, etc (2)
face the noise zone

1 air-intake via the loggia
2 bathrooms
3 noise zone

5

6

8

4 (preceding page) *The living room
1½ floors up from street level, opens
out at its own higher ground level to a
small but extremely well-conceived
low maintenance garden. The dining
space to the right can be closed off by
a sliding wall*

5 *Looking towards the breakfast bar
and kitchen from the dining table*

6 *A view from the staircase leading
from the first-floor entrance hall to the
kitchen and dining-room (ahead), and
the living-room. The glazed screen
(left) is to the lower sitting-room/study*

7 *View of the split-level open-plan
drawing office accommodation. This
can be reached from the residence as
well as from its own external entrance*

8 *Detail of the impressive entrance to
the offices. The door is faced with
blue anodised metal panels*

9 *The living/dining terrace at the
upper ground level (1½ storeys up
from street level), with a full-height
sliding door to the living-room at the
right, and a hinged door to the kitchen
at the left. Note the precise detailing
overall and the external solar control
blind*

10 (overleaf) *Looking down on the
living-room terrace with its most
carefully graded stones and pebbles.
The idea is continued above in the
extension to the second-floor terrace,
also seen in this view*

HILLSIDE RESIDENCE
NEAR STUTTGART

ARCHITECT
Werner Luz

HILLSIDE RESIDENCE NEAR
STUTTGART: Section

First floor plan
1 master bedroom
2 child's bedroom
3 terrace
4 planted roof

Ground floor plan
1 living room
2 dining room
3 studio
4 swimming pool
5 play room
6 snug
7 balcony
8 utility room
9 court

Lower ground floor plan
1 entrance hall
2 general store
3 provision store
4 staff bedroom
5 staff living room
6 guest bedroom
7 staff bedroom
8 boiler room
9 wine cellar

1 *The approach to the house is up this
delightfully landscaped series of
stepped terraces*

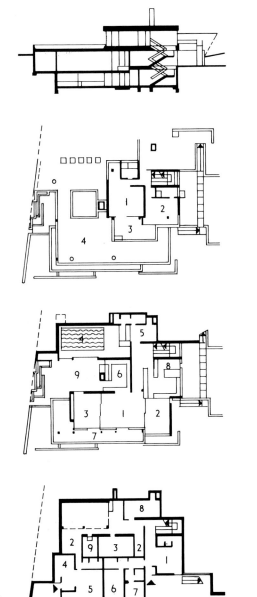

The steep slope of a former vineyard was the site on which architect Professor Werner Luz was commissioned to produce a substantial home for an industrialist client. Full advantage was to be taken of the views over the valley and surrounding countryside and it was therefore necessary for the house to be positioned at a point high up above the motor access road.

To the north the site adjoins a National Trust zone, and in the west a meadow which is not scheduled as building land. To the east the same meadowlan continued, and during the course of buildin planning permission was received for a house on th area too, which Luz was also commissioned to tak on. As a condition as many fruit trees as possible c the site had to remain.

The design of the house on the western part of th site (illustrated here) tries to retain the natur character of the slope as much as possible. Th house has been built into the hillside, the surface which continues on the planted roof. Within a sho time the concrete parapets will be largely hidden b planting. There are two storeys underneath th planted roof, one small one above.

From the road, the approach to the house is up climbing curving 'terrace' of shallow rise concre platforms, set in among carefully controlled, b apparently casual, planting. A long climb whic could easily have been a chore has been landscape into a delightful amble. At the top of this path or arrives at the lowest level of the house and a larg porch. At this level are the guest and domestic sta bedrooms, storage rooms, a wine cellar, the boil room, and entrance hall with cloakroom.

A dog-leg staircase leads from the entrance hall the first floor, the living area. Here are the livin room, music room, dining-room and study. Thes rooms can be made into one large reception space opening two separate sliding walls. Projectin southwards from this long elevation is th balcony/terrace from which the views may be se to best advantage. At the west end, off a par covered court, the indoor swimming pool lies w inside the hill. This court and the living-room a connected by the centrally positioned sunken livin room (or snuggery), used in bad weather, with open fireplace, the massive concrete chimney which also has a hearth to the outside court. T kitchen and its related spaces open towards a yard the east end of the house, from which an extern stair leads up the hill to the terraced kitchen garde On the highest level are the parents' and chil bedrooms. These are surrounded by a small terra and the planted roof which merges into the natu hill.

Various woods, as appropriate, have been used f interior walls, ceilings, window and door frame floors are of black slate or have fitted carpets. T structure overall is of in-situ reinforced concret expressed with a boarded finish. It has be designed by Professor Luz and his team with pleasing visual clarity and simplicity which, togeth with the technical excellence of all the finishes a the beautiful landscaping, has produced the rig ambiance for this industrialist's modern residence

2

3

4

5

6

7

2 The hillside site viewed from the south-east. The lefthand — or west — house is illustrated in this study

3 This view of the master bedroom includes a mirror at the right reflecting, through the west-facing glazing, two of the rooflights to the swimming pool below

4 Detail of the kitchen through the open, horizontally sliding window, with extract hood and louvres. Note the large volume of storage space

5 Lusty 'sea-shore' landscaping seen from the lower-ground floor main entrance terrace, looking west

6 Looking through the partly open double-sliding doors from the swimming pool to the large courtyard, which is carved from the hillside and well sheltered

7 The 16·5 × 5·5 m (54 × 18 ft) long dining/living/music-studio space which can be closed off into three rooms by sliding walls as required. To the right the opening to the sunken bad weather living-room, which can also be closed off by a sliding wall

8 (overleaf) A closer view of the house, built into the hillside. The surface continues onto the grassed and planted roof. The planting will eventually hide the concrete parapets

PROTOTYPE STEPPED-PLATFORM HILL HOUSE

AT RADLETT, HERTFORDSHIRE

ARCHITECTS
Norman Foster, Wendy Foster,
Richard Rogers
Norman Foster now at
Foster Associates

A 1-in-8 north-facing hill just a few miles to the north of London, immediately adjoining green belt open countryside, with good views, was the site chosen by a management consultant and his family for their new home.

The brief to architect Norman Foster was that the house should be flexible in use for the varying needs of entertaining, family living and privacy. It should allow uncomplicated changes in the number of bedrooms, while retaining the same overall volume, and it should also be capable of volumetric expansion with the minimum of difficulty. It should be easy to run and control and easy to keep an eye on the children from the kitchen. Due to the nearness of the neighbouring houses, views to either side of the site were not essential.

The architects' most original solution to the problem of how to satisfy all these requirements was to design the house as a series of stepped platforms following the existing hill slope. The various activity zones of the house were formed by structural brick cross-walls which, narrowing the overall span, allow the use of a lightweight roof deck and top glazing. This top glazing, despite the north slope hill, allows plenty of sun into the house. A system of sliding screens permits simple enlargement or contraction of the kitchen/play/living/dining zones as desired, and the bedroom division walls have been designed as non-structural to allow for possible changes here.

The cross walls dividing the zones extend beyond the end of the spaces on the lowest platform to form 'blinkers' to a sunny and secluded terrace. But this terrace itself could form the start for an extension of the building further down the slope by any one or more of the three contained zones.

The kitchen has been centrally positioned in such a way that there are, remarkably, sight lines to all spaces of the house (except the bedroom zone), even to the terrace and beyond.

It is an aesthetic experience to progress down through the main space of this house from platform to platform through alternating areas of brightness, from the top glazing, and shade, always with the view to the green countryside opening up as one approaches the lowest level.

The drawings show how Foster and his associates have developed the basic ideas behind this house, using it as a prototype, into a viable high density housing system. In this system, services will be carried in prefabricated duct units below the floors, and small landscaped courtyards are incorporated to bring yet more light and interest into abutting houses as they ripple down their hillsides.

1 The lowest platform in use as a sun terrace. Should further accommodation be required, any or all of the three separated zones could be extended outwards

HOUSE, RADLETT: architect's drawing
1 rooflight
2 storage units
3 wall units
4 plumbing unit
5 external unit
6 court
7 precast concrete party wall
8 precast concrete floor
9 circulation over service
10 subsidiary duct

Plan
1 living room
2 dining room
3 study
4 conservatory
5 kitchen
6 playroom
7 bedroom
8 bathroom
9 utility room

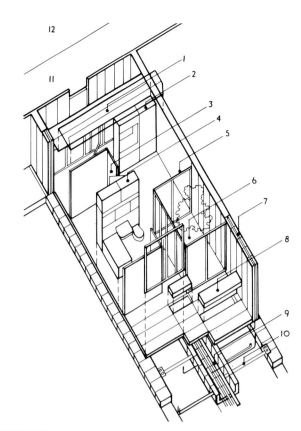

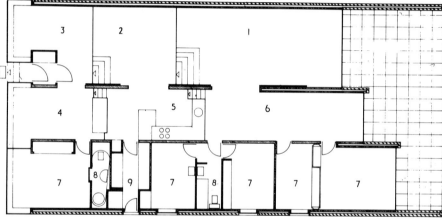

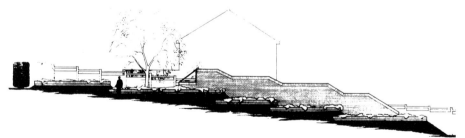

2 (preceding page) *The study on the top platform has this commanding view downwards through the various activity areas on different levels, out to the lower terrace and the countryside beyond. The north-facing top glazing allows plenty of sun to the interior*

3 *Looking over the meadow to the sloping north face of the house, with its terrace*

4 *View of the living room, up through the house. The upper platforms differ in height to match the natural slope of the hill*

5 *A 'compressed' telephoto view of the house from across the valley, revealing the two bands of top glazing*

6 *View to the south front of the house, at the highest platform level. The left sidewall can be seen with its steps following the hill slope*

3

4

5

6

SPLIT-LEVEL RESIDENCE WITH TWIN-COLOURED DOORS

NEAR AALEN

ARCHITECT
Hans Kammerer of Kammerer and Belz

ASSISTANT
Klaus Kucher

Pflaumloch is a village to the north-west of Baden Württemberg near the Bavarian border. It boasts a small high-quality stainless steel tube factory, the owner of which, a bachelor, acquired a plot of building land only a few minutes' walk away from his factory. As architect, he chose Professor Hans Kammerer, giving him as the requirement a design for a substantial house, complete with built-in swimming pool and *Bierstube* (bar). A physically separate smaller dwelling, on the same plot, was required for a housekeeper.

The site was outside the village on the agricultural edge of a post-war residential area consisting of one and two-storey houses. There were, unusually for the quality of house under consideration, no special features about the situation, topography or views which would encourage the design of an outward looking house, and it was therefore decided to create an artificially high 'horizon' around the site by sinking the main garden down as much as half a level below normal ground level. This would also give wind shelter in the rather plateau-like countryside. It was natural to place the swimming pool at the level of this garden, with bedroom accommodation over. As the ground rose gently towards the back of the site, the main living-room/open study was positioned here, a quarter of a level up, opening out — in the summer through floor-to-ceiling glazing — onto a partly covered, landscaped terrace with a cubist waterfall. Opening off the living-room, down three steps, is a snug space with open-hearth fire; a sitting room for cold weather, with glimpses past the partly open chimney breast to the dining-room. Up three steps from the living-room is the entrance level, which contains dining-room, kitchen, utility room, cloakroom, a double garage and a small landscaped courtyard with a massive block of carved stone, set in a pool. From this springs a gentle fountain, which helps to provide a cooling ambiance for the bar which, also at this level, opens off it. Access to the bar can be directly from the main entrance lobby, past the cloakroom and courtyard; it also has a direct access from the kitchen and can therefore be used, independently of the rest of the house, for club gatherings or informal entertaining. The final space on this level, also opening off the main entrance lobby and to the courtyard, is a splendid formal entrance/reception-hall with a small sitting area mainly for business discussions. This hall forms a landing for the staircase which rises half-a-level to the main and guest bedrooms, and goes down half-a-level to the swimming pool, with its changing room, WC, sauna and shower accommodation. Up to half of the glazed swimming pool wall facing the garden can be opened up. A half-level further down

the staircase is the customary cellar space with boiler room, oil storage, wine cellar and general storage.

The materials used were white painted sand-lime bricks for external and internal walls; Oregon pine for eaves, balcony fronts, ceiling boarding and window frames; white Jura marble and fitted carpets on the floors. The roof is covered with several layers of roofing felt, ballasted with gravel.

It is a strikingly impressive house inside; appropriately modest and low lying in its landscape outside; beautifully detailed with a minimum of different materials and put together with the precision of the Mercedes-Benz in the owner's garage.

But perhaps the features which make the residence particularly memorable are the brilliantly coloured, geometrically shaped deep gloss painted designs on the internal doors. Created by the architects, if displayed on a wall, these would stand every chance of being accepted as works of art to a higher standard than many seen today.

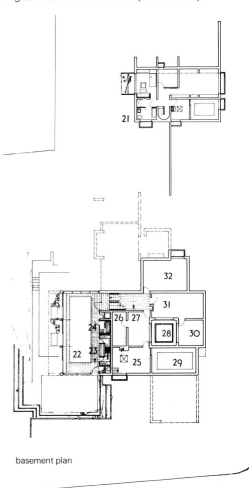

basement plan

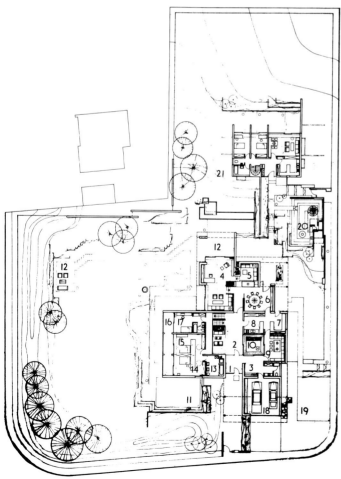

2

1 *The reception hall with staircase baluster in the foreground, a small conference area beyond the planting, and the fountain court of to the left of the painted door. Top right is the gallery to the bedrooms*

2 *Over the oats, the house sits low in the landscape. View from the east of the front entrance and garage elevation, with the two-storey part set back to the left*

3

4

5

6

7

3 *The waterfall terrace at the west end of the house, opening off the living-rooms*

4 *Detail of the purpose-made stainless steel entry-phone/letter delivery box fitment at the front gate*

5 *The smoothly detailed timber staircase leading up to the bedroom floor and down to the swimming pool and extensive cellars. The shot is taken from the reception hall which, in effect, forms a half-landing*

6 *Looking over the desk in the study towards the dining-room (upper left), which can be closed off by a sliding wall. To the right, part of the built-in seating to the living space*

7 *View into the swimming pool from the garden. Two of the deep-gloss painted doors ahead: to the staircase on the left, to the shower on the right*

8 *The fountain court seen from the reception hall. On the right, one of the deep-gloss painted doors, this one to the entrance hall; ahead, across the court, the bar*

9 *Looking from the sunken sitting area to the study zone of the main living area, with its beautifully considered lighting*

STEEL AND PLASTIC ZIP-UP HOUSES
BY WIMBLEDON COMMON

ARCHITECT
Richard & Su Rogers and John
Young in association with Design
Research Unit
Now Richard Rogers & Partners

ENGINEERS
Anthony Hunt & Partners

Wimbledon, centre for international tennis and home of the author, is also lucky enough to harbour a pair of the most technically interesting and visually striking houses in Europe, on a fine residential area site facing the Common. Designed as prototypes for a housing system to be used in both single situations and multiple groupings for the widest social and technical conditions, this commission came from Dr and Mrs Rogers, parents of architect Richard Rogers.

The client requirement was for a two-bedroom house with separate bath or shower rooms for each; living/dining/kitchen spaces; a study/consulting room for Dr Rogers and a pottery for Mrs Rogers who expertly turns beautifully shaped ceramics flecked in pale creamy brown. In addition a small, fully self-contained flat for temporary guest use was also needed.

A programme was evolved with the architects in which it was agreed the following factors were to be taken into consideration in the design: planning flexibility to allow for short-term changes in the size and age of the family and the possibility of different ownership; privacy from neighbours; minimum interference with the natural amenities of the site; speed of building erection; low cost; minimum maintenance.

The solution chosen to provide the most flexible possible space was a structure of eight welded steel rsj portal frames 14 in deep, spanning 45 ft. These were in one group of five for the main accommodation and, separated by an open-sided court, another group of three for the flat and pottery, The Lodge. The frames within the groups were at 11 ft 6 in centres to allow economic production of the factory-manufactured white pvc-faced side wall panels. The same module could be used to enclose the court, should this be required in the future. Under the coating the sandwich panels are 2 in thick, aluminium faced and expanded polystyrene cored. A fast panel-to-panel neoprene zip-up jointing system was used. The avoidance of wet construction after completion of the 6 in reinforced concrete ground slab cut out drying time delays, and with installation by teams of skilled workers employed on a direct labour basis, rapid completion of the walls and roof was achieved.

The roof consists of channel-reinforced woodwool slabs, covered with a high-elasticity polymer-reinforced bitumen roofing membrane. Under this structure is a suspended plaster ceiling stopped at each portal frame to allow this (which, wherever visible is painted bright yellow) to be seen. Small-bore heating forms a part of this ceiling, as do a multitude of little lights set flush with the ceiling.

These give, after dark, a lively sparkle to the various spaces, helped by the seamless white polyurethane flooring laid throughout.

The end walls have been double glazed in full height floor-to-ceiling 8 × 9 ft steel frames, one of which in each wall slides fully open. Other openings in the side panels are standard aluminium framed but doors closing into continuous neoprene sealed openings; all other openings in the panels and the solar reflecting glazed roof sections to the bathrooms are neoprene zipped.

The main house has been designed with a huge living/dining/kitchen space 45 × 26 ft extending from the front to the back of the building with the bedroom study zone given privacy when required by three sliding walls painted lime green. These provide a stimulating visual contrast with the warmer yellow of the bathroom core and other fixed walls, the beams, window blinds and the long shoulder height storage cupboards fronting the kitchen worktop. As a solution to the problem of how to retain the kitchen as an open part of the living zone, yet keep the

1 *A wide-angle view over the kitchen and storage cupboards to the living and dining areas. The sliding walls to the bedroom/study zone are in the background*

ooking activity and clutter out of sight, this one must be ideal. Even the highest piece of kitchen equipment is out of sight from everywhere except behind this gloss chrome-yellow sprayed-enamel and stainless steel fitting. The dining table and chairs were designed in the mid 1930s by the Italian architect Ernesto Rogers (cousin of the owner). The sitting area has chairs from Le Corbusier, Eames and Thonet; a collection of house plants growing near the glazing mellows the strong horizontals of floor and ceiling in this space and forms a good indoor/ outdoor link to the low spread planted and treed courtyard.

As mentioned, the indoor and the exterior walls were designed with flexibility in mind. Due to complications, this is often more a theoretical than a practical possibility. But here the theory has been very thoroughly put into practice in The Lodge. The two plans show most clearly the change which has taken place, from a small flat and pottery and a double car port, to a full-size two-bedroom house for more permanent occupation with a large living-

dining area and secluded but open kitchen off to one side. With the same height of glazing serving only half the depth, front to back, compared with the main house, this space has a tremendously light and airy feel about it all through the day. Again this is assisted by a white floor, here seamless polyester. To reduce the noise of heavy traffic from the major road passing the site, it was decided to raise up and change the location of the high curving earth banking from its previous position. Planted with low maintenance, low spread bushes, this almost hides the houses from the road, and has allowed provision of a sheltered and private sun terrace for The Lodge which makes up for the loss of the view to the Common across the road.

Richard Rogers and Partners are currently working on a major project, the new headquarters in the City of London for Lloyd's of London. It is clear from drawings and models that the design expertise shown in the two houses here, the house in Pill Creek on pages 40-47 and the Centre Pompidou, is progressing very impressively indeed.

3

4

5

2 *The Lodge, south-west elevation, after remodelling. The high planted banking between this building and the road has allowed a space for a secluded sun terrace. The soft green forms of the planting and bank provide a fine balance to the bright yellow crisp lines and rectangles of the structure and blinds*

3 *Looking through the steel portal frames to the car port of The Lodge (as first designed), to the south-west elevation of the main house*

4 *Zip-up houses: the north-east elevation of the Lodge after conversion, seen over the ivy-planted court from the main house*

5 *Zip-up houses: the north-west side elevation of the main house, showing the clean lines of the zip-up neoprene panelling, the zipped-in bus door and ventilation iris*

6 (overleaf) *Night view over the kitchen with the living space to the left*

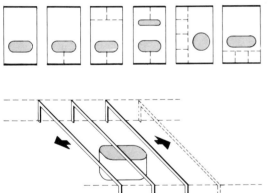

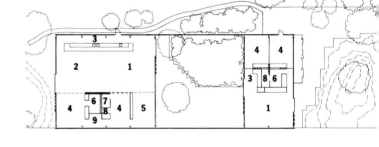

1 living room
2 dining room
3 kitchen
4 bedroom
5 study
6 bathroom
7 WC
8 shower
9 bunk bed

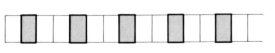

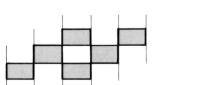

1 living room
2 dining room
3 kitchen
4 bedroom
5 study
6 bathroom
7 WC
8 shower
9 bunk bed
10 pottery
11 car port

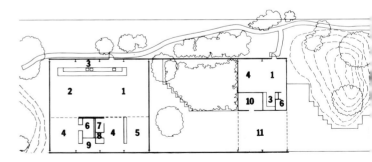

STEEL AND PLASTIC ZIP-UP HOUSES, WIMBLEDON: plans before (bottom) and after (top) alteration

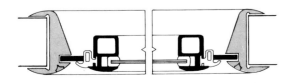

Planning flexibility
Clear span growth service core
Multiple application
Detail of panel-to-panel neoprene zip-up jointing system

8

Similar view to 3. The car port is
ow a spacious living/dining room

9 Detail of the polystyrene
sandwich/neoprene zip-up panel
system with bus-door meter viewing-
window and vent opening

View from the spare bedroom in The
odge, looking past the built-in
itchen to the colourful dining area

10 Front entrance door to the main
house. Note the long elegantly fitted
double 'D' handle

10

CONVERSION OF A 17TH-CENTURY FARM BUILDING

AT CRAVEGGIA, NOVARA

ARCHITECT
Giovanni Simonis

Signora Giuliarosa Riva-Greppi owned a large house not far from a 17th-century farm cowhouse building, half of which had been in her family for a great many years. She wished to buy the other — south-facing — half of this building but was unable to persuade the owner to sell. Nevertheless, both because of the siting of her own half, on the edge but still a part of the lovely old Italian alpine village of Craveggia, and also for economic reasons, she commissioned architect Dr Giovanni Simonis to tackle the major conversion of her cowhouse to a complete home. She instructed that the design should, as far as possible, allow use of her existing furniture, and that the floors overall should be covered with pink ceramic tiles in two tones.

Giovanni Simonis has his main practice in Milan — two minutes' walk from the Castello — but his family home is in one of the villages adjoining Craveggia in the Val Vigezzo. He has, therefore, a natural 'feel' for the local environment, and talks with enthusiasm about the rough stone roof tiling which is a charactristic of the building in this area.

The main problem for the architect was that the building developed vertically on four floors with a plan of only 40 m2 (430 ft2). The original use of these four floors was: cellar/basement level, for cows; ground floor (street level), for goats and other animals; first floor and top floor, as hay lofts.

The house was built on quite a steep slope and access to the three lower floors had therefore been achieved without difficulty from the outside. Inside the house there was only a wooden ladder to the top

hay loft. The architect decided to retain the three level external access and, as the floors were nc partitioned, was able with sheet iron and concret strengthening of the floors to design the ideal interic spaces for Signora Greppi. Two completely nev internal staircases were designed: one from th entrance hall at street level rising gently through th first floor living-room to the top floor; the other down from the kitchen to the lowest level of win cellar, food store, laundry, etc.

The planning solution finally adopted cleverl allows the street level floor to be used as a sel contained living unit when, for economic reasons, i is not wished to heat the entire house or when th stairs must be avoided because of ill health o accident.

The particular position of the house with its fron facing north, built right to the edge of its site whic the stepped footpath hugs around two faces, an close in among the streets of the old village encouraged Giovanni Simonis to emphasise ever possibility of external views. He re-designed th original windows to provide them all with a singl glazed opening, and splayed their reveals, in order t frame the views of a splendid adjoining walle garden, of the massive old church and of th picturesque village lanes and roofs rising up th mountain. On the exterior he aimed to change a little as possible in order to retain the local characte of the building.

Signora Riva-Greppi finds no drawbacks with thi conversion and is very happy with the results.

1 *Looking towards the converted cowhouse (rear half of the centre building) over snow-covered agricultural land, from the south-east. Although the buildings are indeed close together, the distant view gives an exaggerated feeling of this concentration, as can be seen from the site plan*

2 *Top floor: the village of Craveggia climbing up the mountainside, as seen from the north-facing window of the studio*

3 *First floor: south-west corner detail of the living-room. The water-colour paintings are by the owner's father. The old structure of the house can be seen through the window, with the church in the background*

4 *Street level: the galley kitchen, with the top of the staircase down to cellar level (centre right)*

1

3

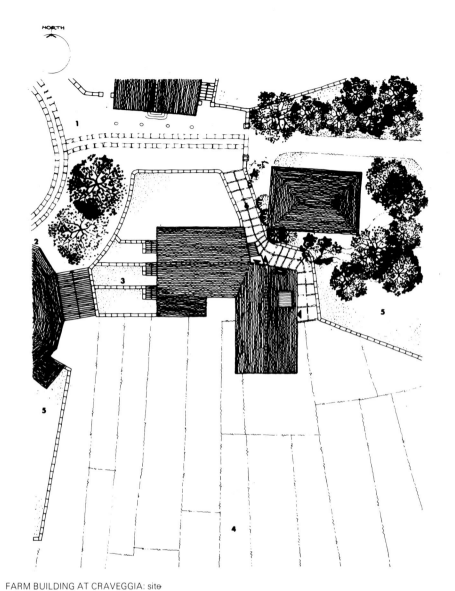

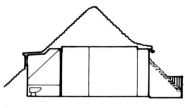

Section BB

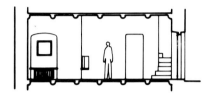

Section of the living room AA

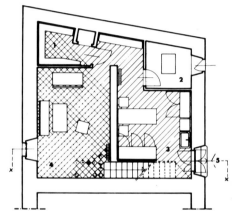

Cellar plan

1 provisions and wine cellar
2 boiler room

3 laundry
4 bar
5 service entrance

FARM BUILDING AT CRAVEGGIA: site plan

1 square of the village
2 church
3 kitchen gardens
4 fields
5 private gardens
6 access lane

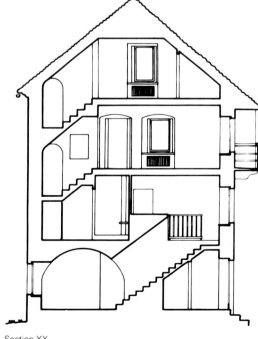

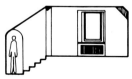

Section CC

Section XX

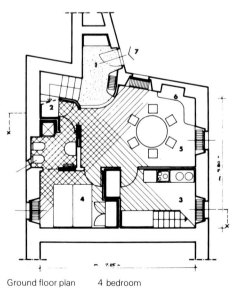

Ground floor plan

1 entrance
2 closet
3 kitchen

4 bedroom
5 dining room
6 fireplace
7 main entrance

7

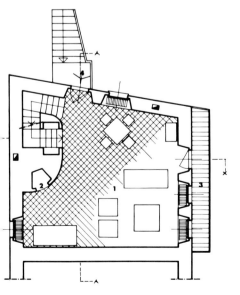

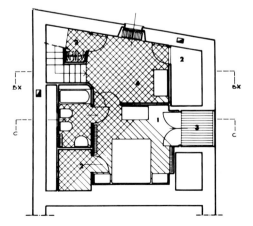

st floor plan

iving room   3 balcony

ireplace   4 secondary entrance

Top floor plan   3 terrace

1 master bedroom   4 studio

2 closet

5 *Cellar level. The cellar bar with its old printing press, and adjoining stores room*

6 *First floor. Looking into the spacious living-room from the balcony doorway. Note the staircase fireplace 'tower'.*

7 *Street level. View of the dining room with the staircase to the first floor living-room, and the entrance hall off to its right*

139

PAVILION HOUSE AND JAPANESE GARDENS

AT SHIPTON-UNDER-WYCHWOOD, OXFORDSHIRE

ARCHITECT
Stout & Litchfield

LANDSCAPE DESIGNER
Alex Rota

This three-bedroom, three-bathroom house designed for a barrister is sited on the edge of the village of Shipton-under-Wychwood in the Cotswolds. It consists of eight separate, linked pavilions. These units are all single-storey and each has its own single-pitch roof. The circulation links have lower flat roofs. Despite the architectural intention to construct the external walls from Cotswold stone and to use single-pitch roofs indigenous to the farming countryside, the design was refused planning permission by the local planning authority on the grounds that it was aesthetically unsuitable. Consent was eventually granted only after considerable delay and a public enquiry.

Throughout the house the roofspace is exposed internally, which gives a most airy and open feel to the volumes. The single-pitch roof was considered to express externally these internal volumes most clearly. Inherent in the use of the separate units are large areas of external wall, which are emphasised by the scale of the stone work. The stone is backed with brick, plastered over a layer of expanded polystyrene insulation and painted white.

As in many traditional farm buildings, in each unit the line of the eaves gutter is the same as that of the beam from which the roof springs. This has enabled floor-to-ceiling window walls to be provided at the front of the units; the rear walls, accordingly, have only one or two small openings pierced through them, again bringing out the solidity of the stonework.

Since the rear walls of the units are not at right angles to the other three, the constant pitch roofs have sloping ridges. This, together with the different relative positions of the units to each other, has produced a fine series of irregularly farm-like, apparently random, changing visual relationships not easily realised from the geometric clarity of the plan. The interior, too, as one moves through the house, has a continuous series of changing vistas to other parts of the interior which frame through the large and small windows superb samples of the—to Western eyes—mysterious gardens outside.

The open timber roofs, glass wool insulated, are boarded, battened and counter battened, felted and covered with Cotswold stone tiles. The timber boarding of the roof and rafters is sealed Columbian Pine; floors are brown quarry tile with electric underfloor heating; all timber for windows, link units and fascias is painted white.

The built-in furniture is of polished beech and concrete blocks or slabs covered with brown quarry tile. A high standard of security was included in the brief for this house, and the architects have solved this awkward problem with exceptional neatness. The fascias, besides holding the eaves gutters, also form a container for fully enclosing metal roll blinds.

Creating a sympathetic environment for the unique house was the problem faced by the landscape designer. Clearly it needed much more than herbaceous borders and lawns. With an early background in the Far East, it was natural for him to consider the Chinese landscape paintings of the Sung period and the gardens they inspired in Japan. He decided firstly to limit his materials to water (a stream fortunately passes through the site), rock, sand, shrubs and moss, all native to the Cotswolds and easily obtainable; and secondly to take his inspiration from the calm Zen gardens, of various periods, which he had studied in Kyoto, the ancient Japanese capital. The Kyoto gardens are recognised as being among the most outstanding creations of Oriental art. They were originated by Zen priests from the 13th century onwards as symbolic miniature versions of the world of nature, and were used for their essential meditative study of man's place in the cosmos.

With the enthusiastic and informed participation of his client, the designer, Alex Rota, over a period of years and clearly with infinite patience, has created seven different Zen gardens to a standard second to none in the western world. That the Cotswold stone house, a little gem of architecture in its own right, sits so well in what could have been an alien landscape is a wonderful achievement, and is helped in no small way by the formation of a lake from which the three bedroom pavilions rise and in which they are reflected.

Here is a house and garden which might well have remained at the drawing stage. One could not have a stronger example of the inflexibility of planning laws which permit pronouncements of absolute dogmatism on aesthetics. If the planning approval laws and their implementation were successful in the reverse direction, that is, if they were to stop poor designs, which are in no way an asset to the environment, from being built, there might still be a case for their retention. It is fortunate indeed that this particular misguided planning refusal was taken to appeal.

1 *An early evening shot of the house from the north. This was the view at a very early stage of the landscaping*

2 *Detail of built-in desk and storage in the study area*

3 *The idyllic water garden, showing the artificial lake, with wildfowl, pebble peninsular, Azaleas, Japanese Maples, bamboo and evergreens. One of the bedroom pavilions can be seen as if rising out of the lake behind the island*

4 *The formal raked sand/rock garden with, straight ahead, the window to the sitting room*

4

5

6

5 *The living-room with its built-in sofa, Eames chairs, and raised fireplace to the right, and far right, a window to the formal raked garden*

6 *Dusk scene. The built-in dining table and seating in the foreground; the island kitchen behind*

7 *The informal sand garden from the main entrance approach. Predominant here is the Canadian Maple.*

7

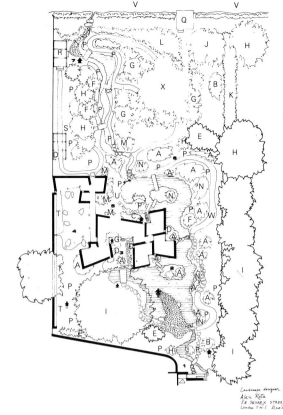

Garden plan

a azaleas

b lilacs

c camelia

d wisteria

e bamboo

f rhus

g Canadian maples

h pines

i chestnut

j oak

k beech hedge

l cherry

m silver birch

n Japanese maples

o magnolia

p moss covered undulating mounds

q fishing platform

r pavilion

s wisteria pergola

t long Zen mural

u outdoor dining area under weeping silver birches

v river

w moss paths

x woodland clearing

1 Entrance garden — moss, rocks, mounds, lantern and stream

2 Water garden — wildfowl, pebble peninsular, azaleas, Japanese maples, bamboo and evergreens

3 Informal sand garden — water-basin, lantern, large maple, wisteria, large magnolia grandiflora, azaleas and 'Blue Diamond'

4 Formal raked sand/rock garden with long Zen abstract mural

5 Camelia garden — moss mounds and silver birch grove

6 Azalea, water and moss garden — path over moss mounds with evergreens and bamboo

7 Tea House garden — pavilion, stream, mounds and azaleas

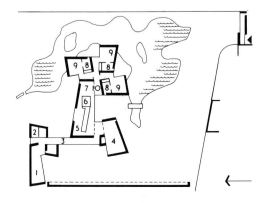

House plan

1 loggia

2 store

3 covered way

4 sitting room

5 kitchen

6 dining area

7 study area

8 bathroom

9 bedroom

10 main entrance

11 entrance from car port

143

LAKESIDE LOG SUMMER HOUSE

NEAR STOCKHOLM

ARCHITECT
Ralph Erskine

ASSISTANT
Vernon J. Gracie

The superb, romantic site of this house is a wooded meadow about 20 (English) miles from Stockholm. It is surrounded by evergreen and birch forest and slopes gently north-west down to the shore of the inland sea, Lake Mälaren. It has fine prospects over the water, to distant islands and also towards the reflections of the low near-arctic summer night sun.

The architect's client is the managing director of a large firm of retailers. He is married and has four children. There were numerous detailed functional requirements for the house, but questions of general disposition, planning and design solutions were left entirely to the architect to solve.

Sweden has a tradition of log building, a material considered to be absolutely right for this site. It was decided to make use of the well established Delacarlia log-building industry techniques. The many small firms in this part of north Sweden fashion and erect the complete timber structures at their factories and the buildings are left, erected, to season. They are then adjusted, and the logs numbered, dismantled, and delivered to their sites, where they are rebuilt in a quite straightforward way. It is, in fact, a good example of semi-prefabricated dry construction which, though somewhat wasteful of timber, is still competitive in cost.

The house was located on the site to make the most of the views, with existing trees and boulders incorporated in the overall design. Excavated material was used to form low mounds protecting against prevailing winds and enhancing the relationship between the building group and its open site. The building plan elements are grouped together, forming an irregular courtyard, protecting this area from winds and close encounters with the elk and roe deer which roam in the surrounding forests.

The structure throughout is 6 in horizontal logs trimmed only along meeting faces and jointed with foam plastic (traditionally moss) insulated internally with 4 in rockwool and lined with large panels of ½ in chipboard veneered with spruce in the general areas, oregon pine in the father's and boy's rooms and aspen in the mother's and girl's rooms. Ceilings are similarly lined. Glued laminated beams shaped to the roof slope span larger spaces; the roof is covered externally with black built-up roofing and chimneys are black painted sheet metal. The maid's cottage/boiler house is basically similar, but the garage is uninsulated and lined with asbestos-cement sheeting.

The windows are patent horizontal-sliding glass sashless units. Despite the construction system, these log structures still have considerable inherent settling movement and must be detailed accordingly.

The wall linings are hung from the top edge and slid behind skirtings, and very large tolerance is allowed at the top of all fittings and wall openings.

The wide terrace towards the lake is cantilevered from the main structure. Canopies and covered ways are formed by extensions of the main beams. Externally the timber is left completely untreated and weathers to a silver-grey.

Ralph Erskine—now of Byker, Newcastle-upon-Tyne fame—started his architectural career in England, sailed an old barge across the North Sea to Stockholm, initially based his new practice in it and

1

hen this grew too big, used the barge every hot wedish summer to ferry his family and staff out to a ooler island in the Stockholm archipelago, where e practice set up camp.

One would expect an architect with such nterprise related to nature to be able to suit his uildings to their environment more than most, and is Ralph Erskine does, the house shown here being fine example. He also has the gift of being able to oduce highly practical but visually appropriate and riking additions to his basic building forms; for cample, hanging balconies which avoid the heat-

loss-bridge of conventional structures, and, in the present study, the tall black chimney which provides that interesting vertical accent to complement the trees and contrast with the long low horizontals of the massive logs.

So, in complete antithesis to the normal Swedish log house requirement for 'peasant romanticism', Ralph Erskine has produced with identical materials and constructional techniques a fine home of completely modern feeling.

1 *The peaceful Lake Mälaren setting of the summer house is seen here from a boat*

2

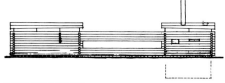

South-east elevation

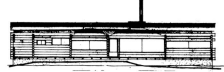

North-west elevation

3

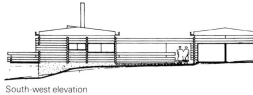

South-west elevation

Section AA

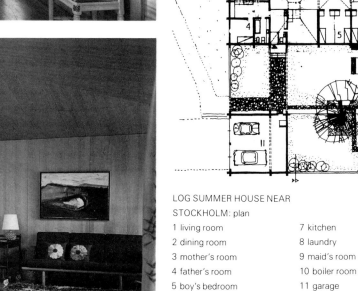

LOG SUMMER HOUSE NEAR
STOCKHOLM: plan

1 living room	7 kitchen
2 dining room	8 laundry
3 mother's room	9 maid's room
4 father's room	10 boiler room
5 boy's bedroom	11 garage
6 girl's bedroom	

4

2 *The terrace, which faces the lake, seen from its south-west end*

3 *View from the living-room to the dining-room, lined with spruce veneered chipboard panels. A glimpse of the kitchen beyond, through the horizontally sliding hatch.*

4 *The living-room seen from the dining-room: the two can be visually separated by curtains. The open-hearth fireplace is also a screen wall for the entrance hall*

5 *View along the north-west face of the house with its cantilevered terrace and roof*

6 *Looking into the grassed court to the south-east of the main house. The routes from house to garage and house to maid's room are delineated*

by continuations of the log structure at roof level, but these are left open, as a massive pergola

7

7 Detail view of the untreated 6 in thick log walling system and the paving, which consists of short lengths of log set vertically and impregnated with arsenic

8 (overleaf) A close view of the long, low north-west elevation to the lake from its meadow garden

ARCHITECT'S OWN REFLECTIVE HOUSE IN LONDON

ARCHITECT
John Guest

Owning a Georgian terrace house in Kensington with a longish garden which backed onto another quiet road, John Guest decided to halve the length of the garden and build a new modern house at its far end. In principle the planning authorities agreed to this project, but in practice it took some two-and-a-half years to gain approval from them and the neighbours for the unique infill design which had been proposed.

Accommodation was required for the architect, his wife who is a doctor, and their two children aged twelve and nine. Allowing for visitors, this meant five bedrooms, three bath or/shower-rooms, a playroom and living, dining and kitchen spaces. For this accommodation a three-storey building was necessary in order to retain a reasonable garden area.

Three floors, three zones: a straightforward division into ground floor for the children and utilities; first floor for living activities and second floor for parents' bedroom and guest bedroom/ studio. However, a planning stipulation was that the house must be kept down to the height of the neighbouring properties. The answer was to sink the ground floor below the pavement level together with the entire rear garden/terrace and a substantial part of the front garden/terrace, thus providing enough height for three main floors and an interesting quarter-level-up entrance hall. From this a stair, delightfully forming an integral part of the house staircase, leads up another quarter level to the main first floor living/dining/kitchen volume. Maximum possible light and space for year-round pleasure in their home environment were requirements of the Guest family in their own brief. Another was an environment which would help them forget the city about them. To achieve assistance in these objectives, the first-floor space has been given floor-to-ceiling glazing on its south-west side wall, its north-west end wall and part of its south-east end wall, which effectively includes the glazed front entrance door. Consequently, at all times of the day and year, the light level is exceptionally high, either from direct sun bouncing off the white 'Iris' ceramic tile flooring (from Milan), or indirectly reflected from the party wall (with its subtle glass mural by the architect) of the adjoining studio house, or softly diffused by the white vertical louvre blinds.

Possibly the major feature here, giving a unique character to the space, is the aluminium helical staircase, partly enclosed in a semi-reflective aluminium cylinder which penetrates exciting through all levels, partly open to give glimpses of the entrance hall with its sparkling aluminium book shelving and of the curved music studio end of the living space with its even more curving Bechstein grand. While the staircase provides visual stimulation, the planted terrace opening off and continuing this living space outside is a most peaceful place. At the south-east end one can look down directly into the small planted pool forming part of the lower front garden; the north-west end is roofed by the extended upper terrace which opens off the second floor master bedroom (used for family sleeping on those rare exceptionally hot nights), and has views down to the formal rear terrace/garden and some big mature trees which minimise the high city skyline.

From the exterior, too, the building has been designed to reflect, in this case its neighbouring buildings and trees, quietly in a handsome crisp grey glass cladding. This reflectivity helps to create an effect of light weight and volume. Like the interior and exterior finishes to floor and terrace (ceramic or marble tile and Norament rubber tile), the cladding was also chosen to keep cleaning simple and major maintenance to a minimum.

The structure of the house is a reinforced concrete frame, upper floors and roof on a concrete pad foundation. External walls are 8 in concrete block clad with toughened float glass panels which have a fired grey enamel paint backing, fixed with putty and stainless steel clips. Internal walls are 4 in concrete block plastered; windows double glazed in aluminium frames. Heating is by two gas-fired boilers one for warm air, one for perimeter grill tube units against the glass. There are four extract fans, in the bathrooms and from the cooker.

Trained at the AA in London, John Guest says that his main influences are the Bauhaus and Le Corbusier; this comes over strongly in the house illustrated here, particularly in the quarter curve of the front elevation, the staircase, the long band of glazing at first floor level. In September 1976, Lance Wright wrote in the *Architectural Review*: '. . . we are strongly tempted to say that this house is not only much better built and finished but also even better conceived than anything the Master (Le Corbusier) did in this line himself'.

Encouragement for all to have patience and persistence in the face of the great planning bureaucracy

1 *Looking down through the rooflight to the reflective aluminium helical staircase and its cylindrical enclosure*

151

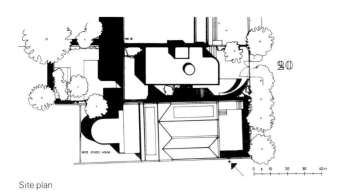
Site plan

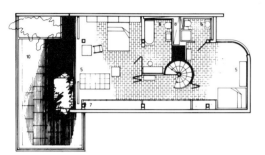
Second floor plan,

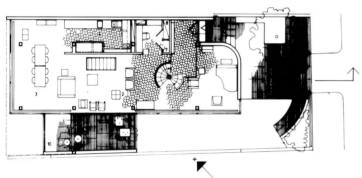
first floor plan

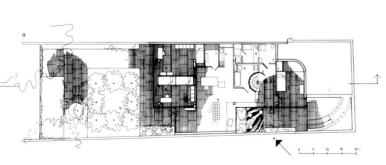

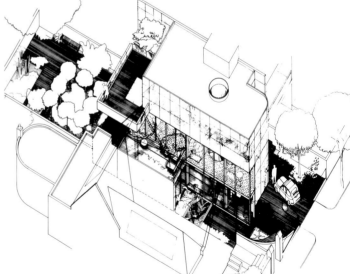
Axonometric

Street elevation

Ground floor plan	4 kitchen	8 services
1 entrance	5 bedroom	9 playroom
2 living-room	6 bathroom	10 garden
3 dining-room	7 storage	

5

2 Night view of the south-east front elevation: to the left is the terrace outside the first floor living-room

3 The sparkle of aluminium in the entrance hall: in purpose-made book shelving and from the staircase with the ingenious use of the entrance hall floor as its quarter landing. Up four steps in the continuing helix is the main living/dining level

4 The main first-floor living space seen from the dining end. The reflective

aluminium staircase cylinder is seen in the centre distance. The space has soft but brilliant lighting, the sun reflected off the Italian ceramic floor tiles

5 Reflective grey backed glass on the end wall of the garden produces an interestingly distorted image of the crisp north-west elevation

6 View of the south-east front, the entrance on the right and the house opposite reflected in the grey glass cladding

6

7 (preceding page) *This night view was shot into the mirror section of a reflective glass mural, by the architect, fitted against the party wall on the terrace outside the main living space. Rotaflex spot lighting adds to the sparkle of this reflective and stimulating house*

8 *Detail of the second floor built-in planter on the main bedroom terrace*

9 *View to the front door with its curving grey glazed wall lead-in. Reflections of the surrounding building vary with the lighting and can be dramatic*

10 *Evening sun on the north-west elevation and formal terrace/garden, largely paved, like the front garden and the ground floor of the house, with Norament rubber tiles. An elevation elegant by any international standard*

11 *A view, well above eye-level, of the south-west side of the house with the lower-ground floor garden and planted pool. A rubber paved ramp curves down to this level from the road level car space*

8

9

10

COPPER-ROOFED HOUSE
AT GREIFENSEE

ARCHITECT
Justus Dahinden

COUNTRY HOUSE AT
GREIFENSEE: plan

1 living area
2 dining area
3 study area
4, 5, 6 staff flat
7 kitchen
8 bedrooms
9 master bedroom
10 court
11 outdoor swimming pool

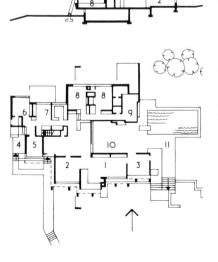

This country house lies on the exposed slope in the National Trust Zone of Greifensee to the east of Zürich, with a splendid view over the lake and towards the distant Alps. The site qualifies as a so-called 'one-family house area' where no large buildings are permitted. It was understood from the beginning by client and architect that the building was to be organically designed, lively and on one floor only, with the mandatory Swiss cellar accommodation. The choice of building materials was also influenced by the orchard-like surrounding landscape.

The house is divided up into three main wings, each serving different functions: living, sleeping and a separate flat for the housekeeper. To the south there is a sheltered atrium court, bordering onto the swimming pool in the garden. The dining area forms the centre of the house and is situated on the open-plan space which links the entrance hall and the living-room, off which lead the bedroom wing and the housekeeper's flat. Its south-facing window wall can be opened completely towards the courtyard with its exterior fireplace.

The very spacious living-room can be divided by two sliding walls and the visual centre is provided by the large open fireplace, its fascia clad with sheet copper, in the middle section. The bedrooms face out towards the rising slope in the east, and to the swimming pool. The housekeeper's flat has its own separate external entrance.

The house is of timber construction on a solid base of boarded concrete; fairfaced red brickwork is used for parts of the interior as well as some of the exterior walls; the roof and its deep fascias are clad with copper. Interior walls are panelled with natural wood; window panes are made of heat-absorbing tinted glass; floors are covered with fitted carpets.

A house which silhouettes with considerable dramatic effect into its gently sloping lawns, it has the immaculate detailing, workmanship and landscaping which one has come to expect in German, and perhaps even more in Swiss, architecture. In this case these facets are complemented by the original design thinking which goes into all the work—including London's Swiss Centre—of Justus Dahinden.

1 *The house from the south. In this view up the stepped path from the entrance to the garden, it looks like some kind of scaly vertebrate resting along the ridge of the hill*

2 (overleaf) *View from the study into the spacious smoothly finished living/dining-room; the latter can be divided off by a sliding wall, as can the study area*

3 (overleaf) *Looking towards the study end of the living space. The sliding wall has a slanted top edge to meet the ceiling when fully closed*

3

4

4 *Detail of the laminated timber roof support beams at the front of the house,* with *a carefully angled* concrete *footing, and crisp detailing* and construction *of the copper fascia,* window, *and concrete base*

5 (overleaf) *To the east, the house in its lawns presents an immaculate and elegant geometrical face; silhouetted against the sky, it reminds us that the Alps are not so far away. An interesting contrast with the multi-pavilion house, Somerton Erleigh, on pages 22-27*

A GERMAN HOUSE

DEDICATED TO FRANK LLOYD WRIGHT

ARCHITECT
Reinhard Gieselmann

The house site in this wine-producing district of southern Germany was a north-westerly slope. It had excellent open views towards a vine-covered hillside, topped by forest and the romantic tower one expects of the classic German landscape.

Specific requirements in the brief were for a well-lit hanging space to exhibit the client's art collection and for full advantage to be taken of views to the north-west.

The architect decided to keep the building with as low a profile as possible on the road side, and it was therefore built into the slope at both floor levels. The building-in impression is strengthened by the terraces of the landscaped garden. This garden, ebulliently flowing with low maintenance planting, was designed by Professor Gunnar Martinson. Visually it complements and softens the geometric structure of the house and is an essential part of the overall design.

The different levels of the house have been established by the design team with great precision. The main frame is 600 mm thick, but it is split in a number of places to allow clerestory lighting. The living-room height is an additional 600 mm, and it too has a 300 mm ribbon of clerestory lighting. Where this clerestory occurs, the ceiling appears to be suspended. At the same time these glazed areas help to produce a well-lit gallery for the art collection.

By means of an irregular cross-shaped semi-open plan incorporating circulation, living and dining areas, the architect has created some fine spaces and vistas. The dining area has been made the centre point of the art gallery, an impressive position for formal entertaining and fun for everyday eating. From the dining area, the gallery narrows in horizontal steps towards a glazed garden door, which is a source of additional lighting and outward viewing. The impression when looking in this direction is that of distance emphasised by apparently narrowing perspective. On looking in the opposite direction towards the little sculpture court — which is really a visual extension of the dining area — a completely contrasting impression of intimate enclosure is given by the close confinement of the asymetric brick wall.

The living/music room has floor-to-ceiling glazing towards the vineyard view, but only a clerestory was felt necessary on the road side to the south-west. At the south-east end, a wide glazed door gives access to a covered terrace on which is positioned a massive, sculptured, in-situ reinforced-concrete fireplace, providing a congenial discussion gallery for cool summer evenings.

A swimming pool has been included in the lower-ground floor, with ceiling height glazed doors

opening up to the garden.

Construction of the building is in sand-lime brick roughcast rendered externally and internally left untreated.

The plan of this house, as can be seen from the architects' drawing, has an existence as composition in its own right, quite separate from the physical building. This is also true of Frank Lloyd Wright's drawings, many of which remained unexecuted as buildings. It is good to see the forceful three-dimensional result of this work dedicated to FLW, by Reinhard Gieselmann.

1 *The lower-ground floor swimming pool. Note the single huge sliding window which opens up half of this wall*

2 *Dusk shot of the open-air fireplace terrace. The figures give an idea of the landscaping scale. The living-room inside/outside detail is shown in view*

3

4

5

6

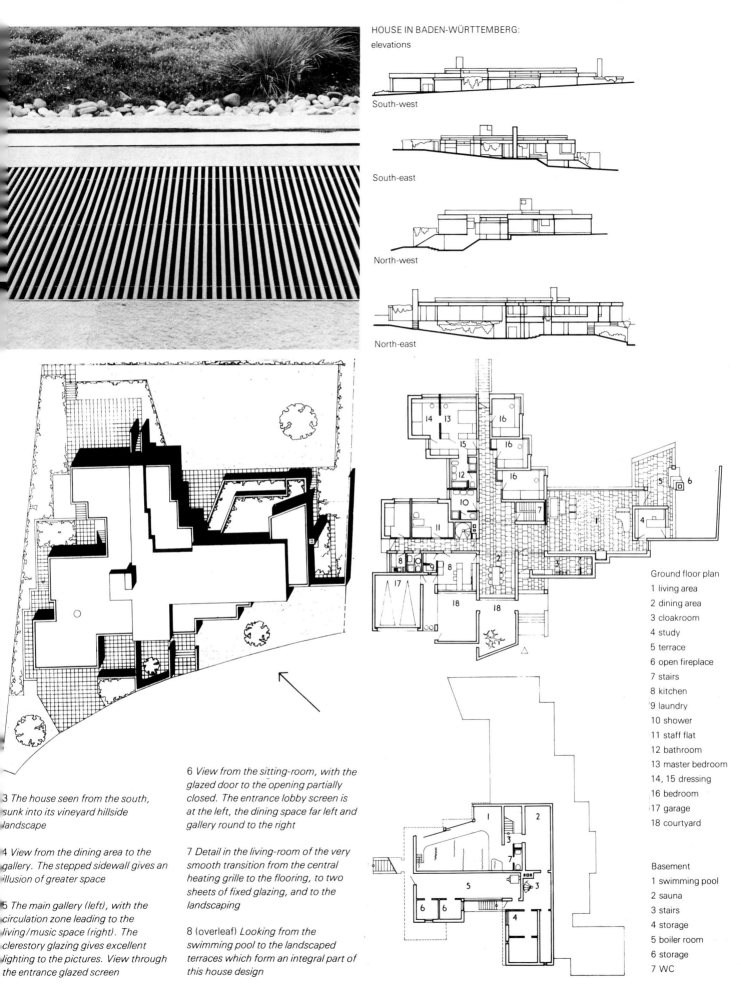

HOUSE IN BADEN-WÜRTTEMBERG:
elevations

South-west

South-east

North-west

North-east

Ground floor plan
1 living area
2 dining area
3 cloakroom
4 study
5 terrace
6 open fireplace
7 stairs
8 kitchen
9 laundry
10 shower
11 staff flat
12 bathroom
13 master bedroom
14, 15 dressing
16 bedroom
17 garage
18 courtyard

Basement
1 swimming pool
2 sauna
3 stairs
4 storage
5 boiler room
6 storage
7 WC

3 The house seen from the south, sunk into its vineyard hillside landscape

4 View from the dining area to the gallery. The stepped sidewall gives an illusion of greater space

5 The main gallery (left), with the circulation zone leading to the living/music space (right). The clerestory glazing gives excellent lighting to the pictures. View through the entrance glazed screen

6 View from the sitting-room, with the glazed door to the opening partially closed. The entrance lobby screen is at the left, the dining space far left and gallery round to the right

7 Detail in the living-room of the very smooth transition from the central heating grille to the flooring, to two sheets of fixed glazing, and to the landscaping

8 (overleaf) Looking from the swimming pool to the landscaped terraces which form an integral part of this house design

MODEL — ARCHITECT'S OWN HOUSE PROJECT

HAMPSTEAD, LONDON

ARCHITECT
Norman Foster
of Foster Associates

The project is more than simply a house for architects Norman and Wendy Foster; it is also a vehicle for exploring the diversity of spaces required by family living and an opportunity to develop new hardware systems.

As children grow older, their needs change, just as the needs of their parents change, with the demands of work and accommodating friends and family. This suggested an approach in which the house is designed to respond to new living patterns rather than inhibit them. The house is flexible enough to provide open or cellular space and could if necessary change to form separate entities around an open courtyard. Even the internal geometries can be free form or rectilinear. In the same open-ended manner, the house can change its material fabric and absorb new products and technologies, whether for reasons of taste or performance or, more likely, both.

The site is part of the old walled rose garden of a large Georgian house in Hampstead, an inner London village some five miles from the West End. Circulation was complicated by legal restrictions, involving the adjoining owners for whom car parking and pedestrian access within the site had to be maintained. In addition, the enclosing garden wall was subject to strict preservation conditions because of its historic interest. By stepping the sloping site, it was possible to house the cars in a "dug-in" garage and provide a lower level route with access through one new opening in the outer wall. The devices of stepped section, garden wall and tree planting all reinforce the separate domains of public/urban/outside and private/garden/inside.

The structure in the version illustrated would be fabricated from high-duty aircraft alloys and provide an overall umbrella with a clear span of 12 m and internal height of 4·8 m. The floor is suspended to provide an undercroft for the passage of services such as waste pipes and heat pumps, as well as the movement of air. Walls, roof and floor consist of movable panels on a common 1·2 m grid. The wall and roof panels are interchangeable so that the proportion of top light to side window can be adjusted according to the internal planning. Panel changes could be effected by two people in a few minutes so that short-term changes could be made as easily as moving furniture around. The structural depth creates a zone for external sun shades or blinds, or into which storage and service units such as bathrooms can be inserted. The under-floor void likewise allows freedom for placing kitchens and bathrooms within the body of the house as well as on the edge. Terraces, sunscreens and windbreaks can extend the house into the garden to dissolve the boundaries of inside/outside; so, too, the garden can penetrate into the house in the form of conservatories or courts.

The model photographs and drawings show the scheme at a particular stage of development. At the time of writing, the structure is under active reconsideration in the light of more recent work on tension structures. Early work on the project emphasised the value of layering the outside walls with varying degrees of transparency, translucency and insulation. Later opportunities to study traditional Japanese architecture and to live in it, albeit briefly, have enabled the architects to rethink their preconceptions and the next stage of design, while following the same basic principles.

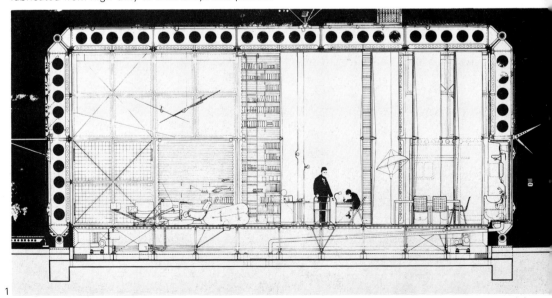

1

1 *Cross section*

2 *Cross section through site*

3 *Exterior view with entrance through the garden wall in the foreground. Note the sunscreens extending the inside outside*

4 *Exterior view from above with entrance ramp in foreground*

5 *Interior view: one is immediately struck by the light, airy feel of this large, flexible space*

6 *Corner detail showing construction system*

7 (overleaf) *A close-up view from the foot of the ramp, with the house sitting on its terrace like a science-fiction structure*

LIST OF ARCHITECTS AND
THEIR ADDRESSES

Peter Aldington of Aldington, Craig &
Collinge
6 High Street
Haddenham
Buckinghamshire
England
Tel. 0844 291228

Arup Associates
Dean House
7 Soho Square
London W1V 6QB
England
Tel. 01 734 8494

Wilfried Beck-Erlang
Planckstrasse 60
7000 Stuttgart
West Germany
Tel. 010 49 711 242331

Justus Dahinden
Heuelstrasse 21
Trigondorf-Doldertal
CH-8032 Zürich
Switzerland
Tel. 010 411 651 478171

Ralph Erskines Arkitektkontor AB
S-170 II Drottningholm
Gustav III Väg
Sweden
Tel. 010 468 7590050

Foster Associates
12-16 Fitzroy Street
London W1P 5AD
England
Tel. 01 637 3611

Reinhard Gieselmann
Seilerstätte 1
Palais Coburg
A1010 Vienna
Austria
Tel. 010 43222 521735

John Guest
211 Coleherne Court
Redcliffe Gardens
London SW5 0DT
England
Tel. 01 373 7920

Hans Kammerer of Kammerer and
Belz
Eugenstrasse 16
7000 Stuttgart-0
West Germany
Tel. 010 49 711 241155/241757

Stephen LeRoith
33 Vicarage Road
London SW14 8RZ
England
Tel. 01 878 3398

Werner Luz
Taubenheimstrasse 76
7000 Stuttgart-Bad Cannstatt
West Germany
Tel. 010 49 711 561427

Michael Manser Associates
8 Hammersmith Broadway
London W6 7AL
England
Tel. 01 741 4381/2

Renzo Piano
Piano & Rice & Associati
Viale G Modugno 22
16156 Genova
Italy
Tel. 010 3910 437325/488919

Ian Ritchie & Jocelyne van den
Bossche
Chrysalis Architects
14 Garford Street
London E14 8JG
England
Tel. 01 515 4989

Richard Rogers & Partners
49 Princes Place
Holland Park
London W11 4QA
England
Tel. 01 221 2828

Giovanni Simonis
Via B Ricasoli 2
20121 Milan
Italy
Tel. 010 392 874073

SOFIREV
6 rue Pillet-Will
75009 Paris
France
Tel. 010 331 742 10 80

Stout & Litchfield
50a Winchester Street
London SW1V 4NH
England
Tel. 01 828 8757

Marco Zanuso
Via Laveno 6
Milan
Italy
Tel. 010 392 866127

DATE DUE